Viscount Wolseley

**The Decline and Fall of Napoleon**

Viscount Wolseley

**The Decline and Fall of Napoleon**

ISBN/EAN: 9783337103651

Printed in Europe, USA, Canada, Australia, Japan

Cover: Foto ©ninafisch / pixelio.de

More available books at **www.hansebooks.com**

# Decline and Fall

OF

# Napoleon

BY

FIELD MARSHAL
VISCOUNT WOLSELEY, K.P.

*WITH PLANS AND ILLUSTRATIONS*

BOSTON
ROBERTS BROTHERS
1895

LONDON:
PRINTED BY WILLIAM CLOWES AND SONS, LIMITED,
STAMFORD STREET AND CHARING CROSS.

# INTRODUCTION.

WHEN the proposal for a series of republications in book form of some of the more important articles and short stories appearing in the pages of the *Pall Mall Magazine* was first made to us by Mr. R. B. Marston, we accepted it without hesitation, perceiving at once that an admirable medium would thus be provided by which much valuable literary matter might be made known to an even wider circle of the public than the readers of the periodical of which we have the conduct. Field-Marshal Viscount Wolseley's graphic, and analytical papers on the "Decline and Fall of Napoleon," which constitute this, the first volume of the PALL MALL MAGAZINE LIBRARY, achieved, as we are able to say from personal knowledge, a very remarkable success not only in England and America, but on the Continent; especially in Paris, where they were translated and published in book form. Much the same may be said with regard to General Lord Roberts' valuable and instructive articles on the "Rise of Wellington," which found especial favour with military readers in all branches of the Service, and we have reason to think that the collection of these into a single and handy volume will meet with the general approval of military men, and might form a valuable text-book for military students. The articles commenced by Viscount Wolseley and continued by Lord Roberts are now being followed in the pages of the *Pall Mall Magazine* by Lieut.-General Sir Evelyn Wood's papers on "Cavalry in the Waterloo Campaign," and we hope from time to time to be able to secure other able military writers as contributors to deal with subjects having an equal historical interest. We conclude by saying that the Publishers have our hearty sympathy and will have our lively co-operation in the publication of the PALL MALL MAGAZINE LIBRARY, and so far as lies in our power we shall endeavour to assist them in making each successive volume such as to entitle it to a foremost place in the literature of the day.

FREDERIC HAMILTON.<br>DOUGLAS STRAIGHT.<br>Editors *Pall Mall Magazine.*

18, CHARING CROSS ROAD.
 *March,* 1895.

# THE DECLINE AND FALL OF NAPOLEON.

## CHAPTER I.

### THE CAMPAIGN OF 1812.

THE expression, "Decline and Fall," adopted as a title for these chapters, seems to imply an unquestioned falling off in Napoleon's brain-power as well as in his bodily vigour towards the end of his marvellous career. From many different sources we have irresistible evidence that upon several occasions during his later years he was subject to periodic attacks of a mysterious malady. Its nature has been variously described; but it was so much his interest and that of those around him to conceal the facts and disguise the symptoms that the world is still ignorant of what the disease really was. On three critical occasions, at least, he was affected by it during the four years of his life with which I propose to deal in these pages. It usually followed upon periods of enormous mental and physical exertion and generally during great exposure. It may, perhaps, be best defined as a sudden attack of lethargy or physical and moral prostration, sometimes accompanied by acute bodily pain. Its effects, as known to lookers-on, were, that at some critical moment of a battle his wonderful power of quick and correct decision seemed to desert him; so much so, that for the time being he almost abandoned the reins to chance.

Throughout his active life he always worked at very high pressure, and so overstrained the machinery of his mind and body that both deteriorated with more than ordinary rapidity. The sword as well as the scabbard showed unmistakable signs of wear-and-tear when they had been only a dozen years in constant use, and the sharp and startling contrast between the manner in which he gave effect to his great plans in his earlier and in his later campaigns is very remarkable.

The most abstemious of young officers had become in 1812 the pampered ruler of a court Oriental in its luxury and had already, at the age of forty-four, impaired his general health by indulgence in its dissipations. Even those who hate his memory will admit that his brain was almost superhuman in its grasp of subjects that interested him. Probably no other man has ever dealt so energetically for an equal number of years, and with such direct responsibility, with so great a variety of involved and complicated public questions of the first magnitude. But, during this process, his clear, nimble brain had suffered from exhausting anxieties and the unceasing work they entailed. His splendid constitution gradually yielded to the frequent exposure and constant fatigues, by night and day, which the peculiar nature of his position imposed upon him.

Beyond all doubt the Republican General Bonaparte who, "rushing down from the Apennines with the rapidity of a torrent," overran Piedmont and Lombardy in 1796 was both mentally and bodily, to a large extent, a different man from the Emperor Napoleon who was defeated at Waterloo. Many careful students of this Colossus amongst men have been compelled—unwillingly perhaps—to admit that had the Corsican general who fought at Rivoli been in command of the French army when it crossed the Sambre in 1815 our "Iron Duke" would not have been allowed to add the "crowning mercy" of Waterloo to the list of his glorious achievements. Nay, more: had it been the Emperor of the "Hundred Days" who assumed command of the army of Italy in 1796 and not the young citizen Bonaparte one feels instinctively that all the brilliant operations of that year in the valleys of the Po the Mincio and the Adige would not have been what they were. Beaulieu and Wurmser might be still gratefully remembered by their countrymen, and whatever peace had been won its terms would not have been so favourable to France as those contained in the Treaty of Campo Formio. As the world flies onwards, with apparently increasing velocity, the sayings, doings, aspirations, even the villanies of this great history-maker are all the more closely studied. A year seldom passes without the publication of some new work about him in which his character, genius, and performances are examined from every side by every sort of thinker and writer; and the more we discover about him and the more we strive to measure his greatness, the vaster, the more infinitely

NAPOLEON.

immense, it seems to be. A superlatively bad man, dishonest and untruthful and whose career embraces some serious mistakes in national policy, whose public life ended in a disastrous defeat and who died in prison, is yet so great a man that his name fills more pages in the world's solemn history than that of any other mortal.

Everything connected with him is deeply interesting, not only to the military student but also to the philosopher and the statesman. No other mortal has been praised and blamed, deified by some and abused by others, as he has been. To men of action prone to worship the great history-makers of the world, he is the most remarkable and the greatest human being who has ever walked this earth; but, at the same time, to a large class of thinkers and philosophers his greatness is merely that of Belial, all "false and hollow." Fashioned from his cradle to rule men and direct events for many years the civilised world rang with his name; and even when in prison nations shook with dread as they contemplated the possibility of his escape from the rock to which they had tied him. He is one of the few great figures in history whom the perspective of time does not cause to dwindle in size or diminish in importance.

Up to the year 1812 he had carried out no war in Europe under his own personal direction which had not been, in the long run, brilliantly successful. From that year onwards he entered upon none which did not end disastrously. By his invasion of Russia in 1812 he lost, almost entirely, the most magnificent army he had ever marshalled under his banners, returning in haste to Paris a solitary fugitive. As the result of his campaign in 1813 he had to lead back the remnants of a beaten army behind the shelter of his own frontier-fortresses. His brilliant operations of 1814 between that frontier and Paris ended in his forced abdication and his acceptance of the little island of Elba as his only dominion; and, having returned to France in 1815 he was hopelessly defeated at Waterloo and sent to spend the remainder of his days at St. Helena.

To what are we to attribute this change in the fortunes of him who had long been the "spoiled child of Victory"? Were his plans faulty or did he fail in their execution? Was the invasion of Russia less ably planned and the wants of his mighty host less carefully provided for than in his invasion of Austria by that wonderful march from Boulogne to Vienna which ended in Austerlitz? Surely not; for the more we study his voluminous correspondence of 1811–12, the more we are struck, not merely with the stupendous nature of the task he undertook when he crossed the Niemen, but with the careful provisions he made for overcoming the difficulties with which that mighty operation bristled. The general scheme was worked out with a splendour of conception and a mastery of detail which, I think, stands unrivalled in the history of the world. And yet the campaign of 1812 was an appalling failure. Nevertheless it is impossible for any careful student of his later campaigns to deny that again and again throughout them he displayed, often in a remarkable manner, his old brilliancy in strategical and tactical combinations and his former supremacy over events.

The invasion of Russia in 1812 was about the most

stupendous undertaking upon which any man has ever ventured. But many are apt to treat it as if its only serious difficulties lay in the nature of the country to be overrun in its very severe winters and in its great distance from the French frontier. At any rate these difficulties have been commonly recognised as the direct causes which led to Napoleon's failure; indeed so much is this the case that Russia seems to have enjoyed a long immunity from invasion because it was in the heart of Russia that Napoleon's first failure occurred. But there were causes other than the difficulties peculiar to military operations in Russia which made well-nigh impossible the task which he had set himself to do.

He did not really wish for a war with his old ally and personal friend, the Czar Alexander. The war was forced upon him as part of the "Continental system" he had designed for the purpose of destroying the commercial prosperity of England. It was, in fact, merely a very important episode in the life-and-death struggle with England upon which he had entered. The destruction of her maritime ascendency — her maritime tyranny he called it — was essential before he could hope for any realisation of the universal dominion he aspired to.* From the battle of Trafalgar, and more especially after the war with Austria in 1809, up to the invasion of Russia his whole energies were directed to effecting the complete

---

\* "La Russie était la dernière ressource de l'Angleterre : il s'agissait de ramener Alexandre au système continental ; la cause était européenne, et toute l'Europe marchait devant moi." —" Napoléon à Ste. Hélène."

exclusion of all British merchandise from every port in Europe. England was apparently the only serious obstacle to his ambition; and, as he had utterly failed in his combinations against her fleet, he now sought to ruin her by the destruction of her commerce.

But her goods still poured into central Europe

ALEXANDER THE FIRST.

through Russian ports; and it consequently became a question whether he should declare war against the Czar or abandon his "Continental system" as a failure. But his pride was involved in the latter alternative; and much as he disliked any breach in the alliance that had been hatched at Tilsit he elected for war. It has been well said, he made "a dispute about tariffs the ground for the greatest military expedition known to authentic history." But the selection of alternatives he then made ended in *his* ruin not in that of England.

War with Russia, for a man in Napoleon's position, meant the invasion of that vast empire, and for it armies were required far beyond the power of France to supply from her own population. He was therefore obliged to depend upon the military forces of Austria, Prussia, and other doubtful allies. He was compelled to lead them through states of ancient military renown whose inhabitants, humbled to the dust in his previous wars, had become bitterly hostile to his armies by whom they had been so cruelly ill-treated. Indeed, his campaigns had begun to carry the conviction into every home throughout central Europe that, however terrible it might be to embark in a war against France it was necessary either to do so or to succumb from misery and starvation.

In his war against British merchandise he had so bullied and irritated European nations, great and small, that not only every Cabinet but almost every family longed for the despot's overthrow, and were prepared to make any sacrifice to that end. In France itself this spirit was alive and began to show itself, for the misery of its people had reached a climax. And yet, whilst England added about three hundred million sterling to her already large national debt during this war against Napoleon, France, under his rule, did not borrow a franc. But the conscription, rigorously enforced, was draining her life-blood, and of the conscripts intended for the "Grand Army" in 1812 some 50,000 had proved so refractory that it was necessary to place them in islands from which they could not escape, until, having been manufactured into soldiers, they were marched off under escort to distant parts of the Empire.

The Marshals, whom Napoleon had created and loaded with riches and honours, were sick of war and wanted to enjoy the result of their labours. They

ST. CYR.

already dreaded his plans for this new and distant conquest. Although French garrisons held all the most important fortresses along the lines of communication between the Rhine and the Vistula, the difficulties of maintaining and protecting those communications were well-known to men like Grouchy, Desaix, St. Cyr, Vandamme, Ney, Davoust, Augereau, Murat, and the others whom he selected for commands in this gigantic enterprise. They were

BONAPARTE AT THE BRIDGE OF ARCOLA.

aware that although the new theatre of war was fertile it was practically without roads and devoid of those towns and villages—the usual centres of population—which enable armies on the march to obtain daily the food and transport they require.

A startling contrast may well be drawn between the abject poverty of the gloomy young Corsican lieutenant, struggling to find food for himself and his brother on his slender pay, and the affluence and luxury of the French Emperor, with Marie Louise by his side, distributing large fortunes amongst his relatives and his newly-created peers. But any such pictures lack the dramatic incidents and stage-like trappings which cling round the contrast between Napoleon as the central figure at the Dresden pageant of May 1812 and as he appeared seven months afterwards, when he arrived at the gates of the Tuileries in a hackney coach by night, fresh from the horrors of his ghastly retreat. The astounding ups and downs in his career are almost as remarkable as his genius. Before the battle of Actium, it is said, that upon one afternoon there were fourteen kings in Antony's reception-room. But at Dresden, upon the occasion I refer to, Napoleon received the homage of nearly all the sovereigns and princes between the Pyrenees and the Carpathians. The Emperor of Austria, the Kings of Prussia and Saxony, the Viceroy of Italy, and many reigning dukes and margraves and ministers of European renown, were there to do him honour, and settle the strength of the various contingents they were to send for the invasion of Russia under his banner.

His published correspondence tells us how he surmounted the diplomatic difficulties he experienced at the outset; and it is an evidence of the skilful elaboration with which he worked out the complex scheme for utilising the resources of states whose rulers and people, he knew, longed for his overthrow. The arrangements he made for repressing with adequate and reliable forces all possible disaffection in his rear when he crossed into Russia are now before us, and those who study his letters must be struck with the care and foresight he bestowed upon the great but disastrous undertaking into which he was led by his pride and an overweening confidence in his "star."

The "Grand Army," which he collected on the Niemen for the invasion of Russia, numbered over half a million of men and consisted of eleven Army Corps,—exclusive of the Old and Young Guard, of four splendid Corps of Cavalry, and of the Austrian contingent of 32,000 men: all included, it was about 600,000 strong, but of these, not more than one-third were French. He took with him over 1200 guns into the field.

To meet this imposing array of invaders the Czar had collected three armies having a total strength of about 215,000 men. There was also, in addition, a fourth Russian army in the field of about 40,000 men, but it was engaged in operations on the Moldavian frontier of Turkey. Napoleon hoped it would there find ample employment and be unable to influence his operations in any way. These were small forces with which to defend "Holy Russia"

THE CORONATION.

against the hosts now arrayed against her under the most renowned captain of any age ; but they were all Russians fired with the deepest enthusiasm, both religious and patriotic, and about to fight on their own soil in defence of everything that man holds most dear.

The French armies were all commanded by well-known generals of proved ability in the field. But the Czar was no great strategist himself, and his generals, unknown to fame as commanders, possessed no special skill in war or aptitude in the movement of troops. At the very outset they had been led into faulty dispositions, the result of false reports spread by Napoleon that he meant to occupy Volhynia. In consequence of these rumours they had scattered their troops over so wide a front that it would be impossible to concentrate them in time to meet any sudden blow from Napoleon. Divided councils the mutual jealousies of generals and uncertain and undigested projects still further tended to confuse and weaken the nature of the resistance they might offer.

Napoleon reached the Niemen at Kovno and crossed it on June 24th. He had long hesitated to take this final step, and would gladly have made peace on easy terms if only Alexander would close his ports to English goods. But at last his mind was made up, and he determined to invade Russia. The faulty distribution of the enemy's forces lent itself to an attack upon their centre. His plan was to force a way through it to Smolensk—then still commonly regarded as the bulwark of the empire—operating in the Polish province of Lithuania where he was sure to meet with many sympathisers.

His passage of the Niemen met with no resistance and the Russians fell back on Smolensk before his advancing troops. This policy of "retreat" was no carefully designed plan, as many have asserted, to lure the French on to their destruction in the roadless wilds of Russia. Under the circumstances the Russian commander could, in fact, do nothing else; for by skilful movements Napoleon with his central force had separated the Russian armies like a wedge well driven home, and he was too strong at all points for any force the Russians could then possibly bring against him. In thus falling back Alexander's generals hoped to concentrate at Smolensk to make a stand there. Public opinion, as far as it could be said to exist then in Russia, cried out loudly for a battle and roundly abused Barclay de Tolly for his Wellingtonian policy of cautious retreat.

Napoleon entered Wilna on June 28th and remained there until July 16th, a loss of time it is impossible to explain away when we remember how late in the year it was when he opened the campaign. Many specious excuses for it have been urged; but it was a fatal mistake if he had mapped out in imagination, as without doubt he had done, the probable course the war was likely to take. This mistake was all the more serious if he meant to advance beyond the Dnieper in the event of his terms being rejected after his first great victory. He calculated upon winning that victory between the upper waters of that river and the Dwina, somewhere on or about the Witepsk-Orcha line.

During his stay at Wilna he evinced an undoubted desire for peace and seems to have realised the danger, if not the unwisdom, of forcing the despot Alexander into the ranks of his active and declared enemies. A want of power over himself to decide such great questions as that of war or peace already began to show itself, and there was an unwonted hesitation, even then, in the policy he followed.

The Polish question now thrust itself most inconveniently before him. In early life all his sympathies —and they were strong then—were with the Poles and he had regarded the partition of their country as a crime which demanded expiation from all who took part in it or shared in the spoil. He knew that the most serious blow he could strike the Czar would be the restoration of Poland and that he could obtain the consent of Austria and Prussia to that measure by giving them equivalents elsewhere for their Polish provinces. As a very young man liberty was his only religion; but he had now learned to hate and to fear that term. The poor and friendless Corsican subaltern could afford to entertain lofty notions about freedom; but the rich and powerful French Emperor, endowed with despotic authority, had forgotten his youthful aspiration in the pursuit of personal ambition. He had no desire, as he put it, to be the Don Quixote of Poland by reconstituting it as a kingdom on those Republican principles which would have alone been acceptable to the Polish nationalists of that day.

Lately received into one of the greatest reigning

houses in Europe he seems to have acquired, with his bride all the royal prejudices of her race, and especially a hatred of republicanism in any form. This feeling was shared by all the kings and princes with whom he now associated on equal terms. In their society he forgot that he had risen from the people and acted as if he had been born in the purple. To fight Russia by the re-establishment of Polish independence was not therefore to be thought of.

Although he hesitated to launch his armies into the heart of Russia the very greatness of the plan he had made for the capture of Moscow seems to have fascinated him. Without doubt he was under the influence of the great successes he had gained in former years. His magnificent victories, and the flattery they brought in their wake, made him believe himself invincible. He remembered how those victories had in every instance given him peace quickly and upon his own terms, and he could see no good reason why a great victory near Smolensk should not similarly cause Alexander to sue for peace.

Napoleon left Wilna on the night of July 16–17th by the St. Petersburg road as if he meant to march upon that city. But it was only a feint, his real object being to make for Witepsk in the hope of catching Barclay in that neighbourhood. Having, therefore, marched about fifty-six miles towards the Russian camp at Drissa he turned off sharp to the right on the evening of the 17th and reached Globokoë the following morning. Having halted there for four days to little purpose he reached Witepsk on July

28th after some unimportant fighting. Barclay de Tolly fell back skilfully before him day by day.

Napoleon's movements had been eminently successful so far, but yet things were not going as smoothly as he had hoped. Portentous storms of rain had for some time overwhelmed his columns on the march and made their progress extremely slow. Encumbered with enormous trains his attempts at forced marches, or even those very rapid movements upon which his strategy was usually largely based, only drove his men by thousands into hospital or left them by tens of thousands as starving stragglers to indicate the route he had followed. The country was exhausted of supplies by the retreating Russians so that it became daily more and more difficult to supply men and horses with food. Prussia, and every province his armies had passed through before crossing the Niemen, had been swept of horses. But the deep mud of the tracks which served for roads in Russia began to destroy them already with alarming rapidity. The unwilling drivers deserted upon every possible opportunity. Even before he reached Wilna he had been compelled by want of horses to leave behind one hundred guns and five hundred waggons.

His advance through the centre of the Russian zone of operations had separated their armies, which, together with their own faulty movements, laid them seriously open to be attacked and destroyed in detail. But his commanders had already begun to quarrel amongst themselves; they would not work cordially together and failed to carry out his best laid plans or give effect to his ablest schemes for the annihilation of the enemy's columns. The first stage of the campaign had been most skilfully thought out and prepared for by the master-mind who directed it, but yet the result was failure. For after some insignificant rear-guard actions the armies of Bagration and of Barclay succeeded in effecting their junction at Smolensk on August 3rd.

It was during the long halt of sixteen days at Witepsk that Napoleon learnt of England's success in negotiating a peace in the north between Russia and Sweden and in the south between Russia and Turkey. Two considerable bodies of Russian troops were thus set free to reinforce the armies then operating on the right and left of the French line of advance. There were, however, vast distances to be traversed by them before they could reach the zone of Napoleon's operations, and he hoped to finish the war before they could bring any direct influence to bear upon his movements. At the same time he naturally felt that they were certain within a calculable period to make themselves felt upon his long line of communications. This should have been to him an additional warning against any advance that year beyond the Dnieper. Hitherto his operations had been in a region where the inhabitants were largely of Polish origin and by no means enthusiastic well-wishers of the House of Romanof. But if he ventured beyond Smolensk he would find himself amongst a purely Russian people deeply imbued with very strong religious and national sentiments, and much excited by the appeals made to their patriotism by Alexander, their Pope as well as King.

Napoleon left Witepsk on August 13th, hoping to fall upon the Russian army before it reached Smolensk and possibly to cut it off from that place.

KING OF ROME.

The torrents of rain which had fallen throughout July were now succeeded by stifling heat, and during the march the dust on the clay roads was intolerable. The rest at Witepsk was grateful to the soldier in such weather, but the losses from sickness and desertions were already appalling. One hundred and fifty thousand of his Grand Army were missing, either dead or in hospital or wandering about the line of communication as stragglers. He knew too well that the farther he penetrated into Russia the greater would become this evil.

On August 16th, 17th, and 18th, there was a good deal of fighting near Smolensk, with great loss on both sides ending in the retreat of the Russians. But Napoleon failed to force his wary adversary into a decisive battle. He found himself in what had been a large city but was now merely a mass of burning ruins—for his shells had set it on fire—where only a small amount of food was forthcoming. The harvest of the previous year had been bad—a fact known to Napoleon before he planned the invasion of Russia—and that of 1812, then being reaped, was either carried off or largely destroyed by the peasants in their flight. They had also driven away most of the cattle and horses, making it difficult for the Intendance to collect what grain there was left in the fields.

What Napoleon wanted and sought for was a great and decisive battle that would enable him to end the war without any farther advance into Russia. But although Barclay was no great general he was too clever to thus play into his adversary's hands. His policy, and it was a sound one in his position, was to engage in rear-guard actions upon every favourable opportunity, as he did at Smolensk, and then, before his army was seriously compromised, to draw off farther into the interior whilst his Cossacks harassed the French columns on the march, swept the country of provisions, and slew the stragglers. In a roadless country, like the Russia of that time, this was certainly Barclay's true policy ; but it did not find favour with his army and was generally denounced in every part of Russia.

Up to this time Napoleon had felt so certain of being able to force on a decisive action before Barclay should get past Smolensk, that he had always held out that place to his soldiers as the farthest limit of the year's campaign. He had striven to console them by describing it as a fine city where they would find rest in the midst of a fertile country teeming with the corn and fruits of an abundant harvest. But they found themselves instead surrounded by burning streets and in a country where the homesteads far and near were in flames.

Throughout, Napoleon's plans had been admirable on paper, but owing to the dilatory and spiritless manner in which those plans had been carried out by his generals he had as yet accomplished nothing of importance. On the other hand, his enemy had succeeded in rectifying the great fault of their original disposition by the concentration of their two principal armies at Smolensk. His lieutenants advised him to halt and not go farther into Russia that year. Behind the Dwina and the Dnieper he could, they said, reorganise his army and establish a new base for another campaign the following summer, should no peace be arranged in the meantime. The serious nature of the enterprise upon which he had embarked was patent to all his marshals and must now, if it had not done so earlier, have come home to him also. But he still believed in his "star" and could not realise the possibility of failure. We can only account for his neglect of all plans to meet the accident of non-success by that overweening confidence in himself and in his luck to which in the end he mostly owed his destruction. When, therefore, failure overtook him it not only surprised him but it found him without any formulated scheme to negative its effects.

He still trusted in the generally accepted opinion that Barclay would soon be forced by the Russian army and people to stand and fight. Besides, the cautious policy his councillors urged upon him did not suit his humour or his reputation. He could not, as yet, brook the idea of taking any public step that might be construed into a confession of failure on his part. He still relied much upon his influence over Alexander to obtain a satisfactory peace whilst he used all his skill to bring about a pitched battle. He could still count upon two months of good weather in which to manœuvre and he felt that such a battle would enable him to crush his enemy, and by that one stroke end the war.

It was not until August 25th that he started from Smolensk with his Guard, the Cavalry under Murat being already for several days close on the enemy's trail. But the horses were in such a miserable condition that little could be expected from them, and Murat did little. From Smolensk to Moscow is about two hundred and fifty miles. The road passes through a fertile country but the retreating Russians had converted it into a desert. The sagacious policy by which Wellington had out-generalled Masséna, when he retreated upon his lines at Torres Vedras, was just then generally held in high esteem amongst strategists. It was closely followed by Barclay as long as he was left in chief command. The French found every village deserted, many of them burned, and all food for man and beast that could not be carried off carefully destroyed.

This policy, however, though fatal to Napoleon was not understood by the better classes and was abominable to the peasantry who were the direct sufferers from it. The cry against the commander became at last too strong to be resisted, and Barclay was replaced by Kutusof who had acquired a great reputation in his wars against the Turks. In accordance with the desire of all classes, civil and military, he resolved to fight a great battle in defence of Moscow, Russia's ancient capital. The position he selected at Borodino was about seventy-five miles west of that city, and he entrenched it strongly; there Napoleon attacked him on September 7th.

The distance from Wilna on the Niemen to Borodino was only about five hundred and twenty miles by the route Napoleon followed. Yet, out of the half-million of men he had with him when on that river, he was only able to place in line at Borodino, for what he believed would be the decisive battle of the war, about 130,000 men. And yet his losses in action up to that time had been insignificant. By drawing in all detachments and many bodies of undisciplined Cossacks and ill-organised militia, the Russian commander had managed to collect an army of about equal strength. There was a considerable proportion of recruits and very young soldiers in the French ranks but the great bulk of Napoleon's troops at Moscow were the finest veterans in Europe and were led by the most experienced officers then alive. But in fighting value the French army suffered seriously from the many nationalities and languages of those who contributed to swell its total. On the other hand, in the Russian army one faith, one language, and one national enthusiasm pervaded the whole. Standing to defend their great historic capital it was quite certain that every man would sell his life dearly in its defence. Under these circumstances a murderous contest was to be expected; the result fulfilled popular anticipation for the battle of Borodino was perhaps the bloodiest in modern history.

As subsequently at Waterloo, Napoleon was overjoyed at finding that his enemy meant to stand for a great pitched battle, especially as the original distribution of the Russian army at Borodino gave him every promise of inflicting a crushing defeat upon it. He made his arrangements for an attack upon the Russian left which if successful would enable him to cut off the enemy from Moscow and drive their centre into the river upon which Borodino stands.

According to all the best conceptions of the general's science nothing could be more perfectly conceived or in design better elaborated than Napoleon's plan of attack; but from a variety of causes the execution was poor and unsuccessful. One of those causes was an overwhelming attack of his mysterious malady at the most critical period of the battle. It occurred when Ney, having gained a great success, only required prompt and sufficient support to have made Borodino a great and most probably a decisive victory. But instead of being so it merely ended in the utter exhaustion of both sides, whilst some 80,000 dead and wounded covered the field. The Russians retreated; but they left neither gun nor standard behind as a trophy in the hands of the French. This battle gave Moscow to the French; but when we fully consider Napoleon's position at the moment it seems to me that the Russians really gained more by it than the French.

Napoleon entered Moscow on September 14th. The pillage and burning of that picturesque city is a well-known story. It has been graphically told by the historians of many nations; its dramatic incidents have furnished the romance-writer with many a plot and still supply the artist with endless subjects for his pen and brush. Want of space prevents me from dwelling upon it; but Napoleon's fatal delay in that city cannot be passed over without remark. It was that delay, coming upon the time lost at Wilna, Globokoë, and Witepsk, which determined the fate of his army and, as some argue with much force, his own downfall also.

He made some serious mistakes in his calculations about this Russian war—the date when the rigorous winter might be expected, for example; but the great blunder which runs through all his actions in this campaign was his misconception of the Czar Alexander's character. This is a curious fact; for Napoleon knew him well and had numerous opportunities for gauging his ability, temperament, aims, and what were the strongest forces that worked within him to influence his actions. But although I believe Napoleon to have been by far the greatest of all great men, he has always struck me as having been a bad judge of character. Like many other rulers and generals he did not care to surround himself with very clever or brilliant assistants and he often made serious mistakes in the selection of men to do his bidding. In this respect he was, I think, inferior to Marlborough who seems to have understood not only the thoughts of those he personally dealt with but to have known by intuition even the manner in which they would give effect to his or to their own projects.

Be this as it may Napoleon certainly misread Alexander's character, and lingered on in Moscow under the delusion that his prolonged stay there would bring the Czar to terms; in this belief he was encouraged by the wily Kutusof. His army was rapidly falling off in numbers, whilst the Russian armies were being constantly reinforced. His delay gave time for the main Russian army to recover from the effects of Borodino and to take up a position about forty miles south-west of Moscow which threatened Napoleon's line of retreat. It gave the army of Finland time to approach the zone of operations and the army of Tchichagof, from the south, to do so likewise. Above all it brought on still nearer the dreaded winter, the greatest enemy of all. The one thing it did not bring was any answer from the Czar beyond the statement that he refused to negotiate as long as his enemy was on Russian soil.

It was, I think, a fatal error of Napoleon to have advanced beyond Smolensk in 1812. But he might have retrieved it in a great measure if, after an interval sufficient to prove his assured possession of Moscow and to rest his army there, he had forthwith begun his return march upon Smolensk. He could have effected his retreat without difficulty up to September 21st, or even a few days later; for he might then have selected a line through districts that had not been devastated. He might have chosen his winter quarters so as to be within reach of his magazines, whilst he continued to threaten Russia with a fresh invasion the following year. He would have left her for the present with her ancient capital destroyed, many of her best towns ruined, and the impotence of her generals and armies to resist his advance clearly demonstrated to the world.

Napoleon did not leave Moscow until October 19th. The winter was already upon him and there had even been a premature fall of snow a week before the city was evacuated. His army was still somewhat over 90,000 strong but it was encumbered with trains of waggons laden with loot. Had Napoleon burned every article pillaged from the capital and filled the carts so emptied with food, the march would have been greatly accelerated. Thousands would have been saved of those who died of want.

I cannot dwell upon the details of this disastrous retreat though it teems with incidents deserving of notice. It is one of the most dreadful events in military history and its story can never fail to interest all mankind. Suffice it to say, that indis-

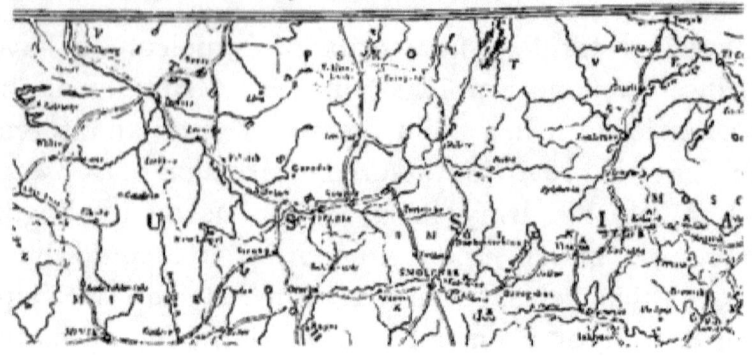

A MAP exhibiting the Retreat of the FRENCH ARMY from MOSCOW to PARIS.

cipline in its most hideous form soon set in with all its fatal results. Some time before Napoleon reached Smolensk—November 9th—the Grand Army had been diminished by half the numbers which had quitted Moscow three weeks before. The horses perished so rapidly that guns were almost daily left behind for want of means to draw them. A strange want of foresight on the part of Napoleon was his neglect to make provision for rough-shoeing the horses, to enable them to keep their feet over the frozen roads. This neglect had no small influence upon the horrors of the disaster which overtook his army.

By the time the Beresina was reached the retreating mass had degenerated into mobs made up of thousands of men, mostly unarmed, who had once been soldiers but who would not then even face the enemy or obey any orders. Their rear and flanks were covered by small fighting divisions in which the proportion of officers was many times greater than usual. These small bodies of determined men alone retained any fighting formation or even the semblance of soldiers.

At Smorgoni, on December 5th, Napoleon made up his mind that his only hope of saving the empire lay in his rapid return to France. There he would raise a new army, and by lying bulletins try and make the world forget his disasters in glowing descriptions of fabulous victories achieved between the Niemen and the Moskwa. He transferred the supreme command to Murat, who, three days afterwards, brought the remains of the Grand Army into Wilna. When Kovno was reached its fighting strength was scarcely six thousand armed men. The passage of the river was signalised by a feat of arms, which is remarkable even among the many in Ney's career. Covering the retreat across the Niemen with a mere handful of gallant soldiers sustained by his splendid example, he found himself at last in Kovno

MURAT.

with a party of only thirty or forty men and the bridge over the river in possession of the enemy. Seizing a musket he led this little band of heroes to the attack, cleared the bridge and once more rejoined the army to be again its protector against the Cossacks who still swarmed round its rear guard.

Later on the arrival of some fresh troops from

Italy enabled Eugène de Beauharnais to lead back behind the Elbe the wretched remains of what could then only be called in irony "The Grand Army." Ney, "the bravest of the brave,"—a proud name even amongst the many which adorn the history of France —covered himself with honour and glory when in

NEY.

command of the rear-guard during the appalling disasters of this retreat from Moscow. His daring courage will be for ever the admiration of all Peoples who still preserve any national sentiment for the self-sacrificing soldier who counts his life as dross in comparison with the upholding of his country's honour. As we read of Ney's chivalrous conduct throughout this campaign we cannot help feeling what poor creatures many of Homer's fabulous heroes were when compared with him.

The invasion of Russia ended in disastrous failure. Those who like may attribute this fact to mere ill-luck on Napoleon's part ; but to me it seems truer to say, that he was no longer the leader he had been in his early campaigns and that his great work was done. He had destroyed the rotten remains of systems which had lingered on in Europe from the middle ages. Though as Emperor he may have sought to revive some of them, what he had done in the plenitude of his power rendered hopeless any attempt to restore them except artificially and even then with the certainty that they must soon disappear altogether. But it was time that his own despotism should pass away. It pressed too heavily upon the civilised world and it was essential for human interests that Europe should once more breathe freely. The decree from above had gone forth against him, and as ill-luck it was recognised by himself when he said that his star was no longer in the ascendant.

## CHAPTER II.

### THE CAMPAIGN OF 1813.

It will be remembered that it was on December 5th, 1812, that Napoleon left his army at Smorgoni, bent upon making for Paris with all possible speed. It is not my intention, in these pages, to follow the fortunes of the "Grand Army" after he had quitted it. All ranks felt his departure to be a fresh calamity that had overtaken them. As long as he was with the army, so great was their faith in him as a leader, they believed he would eventually save them. The feeling of personal devotion with which he had inspired them exercised a strong influence over their discipline and fighting power. But as soon as it became widely known that he was no longer present to command them in action and to chide them when they failed in any duty, despair seemed to take possession of their minds and to enfeeble their bodily strength. Thenceforward all orders were disregarded, and Murat, their nominal commander-in-chief, could no longer control their actions or enforce his authority. Even his subordinate generals refused to obey him. The men did as they pleased, and absolute ruin was the result. "A general recklessness confounded all ranks, command ceased, and it became a *sauve-qui-peut* at a funeral pace." *

When bidding good-bye to his generals at Smorgoni, Napoleon promised to rejoin them in the early summer with a new army of 300,000 men. The Austrian and Prussian contingents to the right and left of the Grand Army had not been seriously engaged in Russia, and he calculated that the remains of the Grand Army, when joined by the reserves collected between the Oder and the Elbe, would amount to about 200,000 men. He therefore hoped to appear again on the Vistula with an imposing force of nearly half a million of soldiers. But as far as his Allies were concerned he was soon undeceived. The Prussians, under General York, entered into a convention with the Russians at the end of December, and the Austrians, under Schwarzenberg, fell back towards Galicia without any attempt to resist the Czar's advance.

Napoleon had hoped that the remains of the Grand Army would be able to hold its own on the Vistula until he should be in a position to rejoin it with a large reinforcement in the summer. But this defection of his Allies rendered that impossible. Prince Eugène Beauharnais, who had succeeded Murat as commander-in-chief, soon found himself compelled to withdraw to the Elbe, having first thrown strong garrisons into the fortresses on the Oder and the Vistula.

It took some little time for the world outside Russia to realise the completeness of the Moscow disaster; but when it became generally understood a

* Sir Robert Wilson.

revival, at least an outward expression of national enthusiasm, showed itself daily more and more throughout Germany and the states of Central Europe.

The conviction arose all along the line that the moment had come when the cruel yoke under which they had so long groaned might be effectually thrown off; and this feeling was deeper and more general in the houses of the middle classes than in the cabinets of kings and statesmen. The many principalities which Napoleon had formed into the Confederation of the Rhine, as well as other allied powers, already began to secretly negotiate with England and Russia to accomplish his overthrow; the terror of his name as yet prevented them from openly declaring against him. So much was this the case, that for some time even the defection of York's contingent was disavowed by the King of Prussia as the unauthorised act of that general. Austria still professed to be his ally and protesting against the defection of others assured him that her negotiations with his enemies were undertaken in his interests. But the states of Central Europe were already honeycombed with secret societies whose moving influence was personal hatred to Napoleon and detestation of the system he had imposed upon Europe. Day by day their kings and princes were urged to declare themselves against the common enemy, and the angry passions of the people, thus aroused, hastened the inevitable result.

Wellington said that Napoleon at the beginning of 1812 governed one half of Europe directly and almost all the other half indirectly. To shake off completely the dread in which his name was held could not therefore be accomplished in a moment, and it took some little time before even the knowledge of his Russian catastrophe drove the conviction into the hearts of his nominal allies that he was vulnerable, like all other mortals. However, before Napoleon was again able to take the field in Germany, Prussia, urged on by the Czar, plucked up courage to openly declare against him, and his father-in-law, the Emperor Francis, announced that Austria would assume a position of armed neutrality.

But meanwhile Napoleon in Paris was not idle. Day and night he worked hard at the creation and organisation of a new army that should restore his renown which had been so seriously shaken by the recent disasters. At no previous period of his career did his commanding genius, his colossal power of work, his capacity for organisation—both civil and military—his wisdom, in fact, shine out more conspicuously. No other man could have accomplished what he did in that dreary winter. The result of all these labours was, that by April 25th, 1813, he was able to take the field with a new army of 140,000 men well equipped with guns and every fighting requisite. This army rendezvoused at Erfurth, Weimar, Gotha, Saalfeld, and Coburg. His one weak point was his cavalry for which he could not obtain a sufficient number of suitable horses.

In the meantime the remains of the Grand Army under Eugène had been largely reinforced, and, now numbering some 40,000, was collected at and round Magdeburg. The corps of Davoust, not yet very strong, was between Tougau and Dessau, and that of Victor was between Magdeburg and the Saale. Behind these forces his new army was being organised in France with all possible speed and was able to join hands with them before the end of April.

From the date of his return to Paris until he was

EUGÈNE BEAUHARNAIS.

again in the field with his newly raised but yet formidable army was only four months : almost an incredible achievement. Europe had assumed that the old and dreaded war-lion was no more or at least wounded to the death ; and great, therefore, was the astonishment of all nations when this new army sprang from the ground, as it were, at his command.

But to make it up he was compelled to draw largely upon his armies in Spain for old soldiers to leaven the newly raised mass, and whole regiments of well-seasoned Marines were incorporated in it with the same object. Although the great bulk were immature men imperfectly trained as soldiers, he had the great advantage of possessing, left from the wreck of the "Grand Army" of Russia, a large number of experienced officers who were of incalculable value in the organization of this new army. But still it could not be compared for marching or for fighting power with his armies of Austerlitz or of Jena. Of the generals in command of divisions, few were capable of handling large numbers of men in action; indeed, his letters of this period teem with complaints of their inefficiency.

To raise and equip an army in 1813 was, however, a much simpler operation than it would be at the present time. All the implements and weapons of destruction then were of the simplest kind. No complex machinery was required for their construction, and the repair of those injured in the field was an easy matter. In those days you could almost cut down a tree to-day, and by to-morrow have it converted into a gun carriage, and the guns themselves could be cast by the hundred with the greatest rapidity. Besides, the soldier then had comparatively little to learn. No months spent on ranges were required to teach him to shoot. He loaded his primitive firelock as our musketeers had done theirs at Sedgemoor, and, like them, fired it straight to his front at any enemy within a hundred and fifty yards distance. No long and careful training in attack formations was necessary to teach him to face clouds of shrapnel bullets and the hail of close rifle fire which the assailant has now to advance through. A battle was not then the appalling convulsion, the terror-striking trial to the nerves and to a man's instinct of self-preservation, that it is in these days of great explosives and of arms of precision. The regimental officer then had himself little to learn beyond what came naturally to the English country gentleman. The tactics were of the simplest sort. Fire discipline was then as unknown as the art of photography, and the officer's chief duty was to lead his men straight upon the enemy. The military system of every great European power at this moment rises in evidence to protest against the theory of the British optimist on this subject. In the Confederate war of 1861–65 great quickly raised armies fought well against armies similarly constituted and equally undisciplined and untrained. It is often therefore urged, by men who know nothing of war, that in case of invasion we too could in like manner put hundreds of thousands of men in the field who would save us. The civilian is prone to forget that our hastily improvised army would have to meet a thoroughly organized army of regular troops. You might just as well hope to win the Derby with an imperfectly trained horse as to win a battle with partially trained, ill-disciplined levies against an army of regular soldiers.

The reappearance of Napoleon towards the end of April in the heart of Germany with a new army took the Allies by surprise, and they had yet to learn how formidable that army could be under his leadership. They had made up their minds that, after the annihilation of his enormous army in Russia, Napoleon would never again be in a position to cross their path. But here he was once more, apparently as vigorous as ever, barring their advance, and ready to spring at the throat of the first army he met.

Kutosof had fallen a victim to the malignant fever then devastating the districts traversed by the retreating French army as it starved "exhausted regions in its way." He had been replaced by Wittgenstein.

It was exceedingly important to the cause of the Allies that their troops should be pushed forward as soon and as far as possible in order to give confidence to the country people, then only too anxious for an opportunity of joining their standards. The armies of the Allied powers had all suffered more or less in the previous year's operations and their numbers was consequently not what they had been. Their strength was still further reduced by the strong detachments it was necessary to leave behind to watch the French garrisons in the Prussian fortresses. The result of this attempt to cover as much ground as possible, in order to inspire general confidence, was that the Allied Armies advanced in far too scattered fractions. Their great enemy was consequently amongst them in strength superior to theirs at all important points before they even knew for certain that he had any new army at all with which he could take the field.

On May 1st, as Napoleon was pushing forward to seize Leipzig, his troops had a trifling skirmish with the Russian advanced-guard. Although this somewhat opened the eyes of the Allies to the fact that they had a regular army as an enemy on their path, they still refused to believe that it was an efficiently trained force or that Napoleon could possibly be again in the field with the numbers he had actually with him. Wittgenstein persisted in believing that he had to deal only with a comparatively insignificant army almost exclusively composed of recently enrolled young conscripts. So strong was this conviction that he assumed the offensive hoping to surprise the French on the march. With this object in view, he pushed forward to Lutzen at the head of about seventy thousand men and suddenly found himself in the midst of Napoleon's army. The battle of May 2nd, known by the name of that city, was the outcome of these movements, and the eyes of the Russian general were soon opened to the great mistake he had made. Although the nature of his offensive movement gave him some advantage at the earlier stages of the battle he was soon heavily repulsed by the troops whom Napoleon had thoroughly in hand. The battle was indecisive, but Wittgenstein's position the day after was so obviously faulty and dangerous that he was glad to escape from it by a rapid retreat. The Emperor's weakness in cavalry prevented any effective pursuit, and the defeated Allies fell back in safety behind the Elbe.

This battle, the first of the year, though without any decisive result—indeed, a rather doubtful French victory—was yet sufficient to inspire Napoleon's young soldiers with a spirit of confidence when they found themselves pursuing an enemy who had so lately driven the Grand Army out of Russia.

By May 8th the Allies had fallen back to the strong position of Bautzen and Napoleon had made a triumphant entry into Dresden, the home of his faithful ally

a. *Position of French Army on October 16.*
b. *Position of French Army on October 18.*

PLAN OF THE BATTLES OF LEIPZIG ON THE 16TH AND 18TH OCTOBER, 1813.

C. *Russian Army.*
D. *Austrian Army.*
E. *Prussian Army.*
F. *Swedish Army.*

the King of Saxony. That monarch, who had been hard pressed by the Austrians to abandon his friend, now returned to his capital. Although the heart of his people was in the great German movement against the French Emperor, he was able, by his personal influence, to place the whole resources of his kingdom at Napoleon's disposal. For the time, at least, this checked the contagion of desertion from the French alliance.

This occupation of Dresden, together with Ney's capture of Torgau and that of Hamburg by Davoust, placed the line of the Elbe once more in Napoleon's hands.

It is a remarkable feature in the decline of Napoleon's fortune that he won many battles where he only just missed gaining the decisive success that would in all probability have restored his position in Europe. The last day's battle near Smolensk, in the previous year, is a case in point. It might, it ought to have ended in the complete destruction of Barclay's army; and had it done so, it would most probably have insured peace on terms in every way acceptable to the French Emperor. The battle of Bautzen, which now followed, is another instance.

The Allies, about 150,000 strong, had taken up a very strong position, with their left resting on the Bohemian mountains, and had strongly fortified it. It had, however, one most serious defect: there was only one line of retreat from it. This, Napoleon's quick eye took in at once, and he laid his plans accordingly. His intention was to assail it in front himself with about 80,000 men whilst Ney with about 70,000 more should fall upon the right flank and rear of the Allies to cut them off from their only line of retreat. But the handwriting on the wall had already condemned Napoleon to eventual destruction; and here, as throughout the remaining events of his career, the cup of success was dashed from his lips just as he essayed to drink from it. Ney failed to carry out the mission entrusted to him and which in the morning he had started to execute. The Prussians held the right of the Allied position. Blucher, who commanded them, had detached a small force of infantry and artillery to protect his rear, and with it Ney became engaged. Instead of pressing his march along the rear of the Allied Army to cut off its retreat and attack it in rear whilst Napoleon assailed it in front, Ney allowed his movement to be checked and his direction diverted by this insignificant Prussian detachment. This fighting soon roused Blucher to a sense of his extreme danger and he at once fell back and made good his retreat. Barclay with his Russians took up the duties of a rearguard, and, having shown a good front to his enemy as long as daylight lasted, he also got safely away during the night. It was entirely Ney's fault that the Prussian and the Russian armies were thus able to escape from the snare so well devised by Napoleon to catch them in. It must be remembered that the French army was quite half again as strong as theirs was. Such are the uncertainties of war even when waged under the personal direction of so great a captain as Napoleon. Ney, in fact, had only succeeded in manœuvring the Allies out of a position in which Napoleon intended to destroy them and where they must have been destroyed had his orders been skilfully obeyed. Had the Emperor left Ney to attack in front whilst he himself directed the turning movement, Bautzen would doubtless have been one of the most complete victories he ever gained. Indeed, it is hardly possible to doubt that he would have almost regained at a blow his former position in Europe. The whole available force of the Russians and Prussians within the region of operations would have been hopelessly broken up. Austria, which was waiting to see which way victory inclined, would have held back from the Alliance against him; he could then have easily crushed the troops being collected at Berlin, and the provinces that subsequently became the recruiting ground for armies to be employed against him would have remained subject, being held in subjection by his triumphant legions.

Both Lutzen and Bautzen were bloody contests for the two contending sides yet neither led to any decisive result. Well indeed may the baffled Emperor have cried in anger, "What a massacre for nothing!" Although the Allies again made good their retreat after the battle of Bautzen, both it and Lutzen were held to be substantial French victories in the general estimation of Europe. They reasserted Napoleon's military ascendency and weakened the influence of the secret societies which were then in full blast throughout Central Europe. These societies worked hard to dissolve the Confederation of the Rhine and to accomplish the Emperor's downfall. Every allied army is weak through the national jealousy of the troops employed—a feeling which is often seriously heightened by the envious rivalry of their respective leaders. In this instance an angry spirit had already grown up between the two allies then in the field. The Prussians attributed their defeat to Wittgenstein's want of ability, and the Russians began to murmur at having to fight battles in defence of Prussian territory.

The natural and safe line of retreat for the allied

BERNADOTTE.

Prussian and Russian army would have been northwards, towards Prussia and Poland. To retreat in an easterly direction to Silesia, along the Austrian frontier, was certain destruction if Austria were really and honestly neutral as she still professed to be. Such a line of retreat would have enabled Napoleon to drive them into Austrian territory. Viewing the tortuous policy which then characterised the Cabinet of Vienna, it is difficult to guess what would have happened had Napoleon by a rapid pursuit driven the Russo-Prussian army into Bohemia. This would have forced Austria's hand, a result which she was most anxious to avoid as she still desired above all things to gain time. As long as she professed to be a neutral power she would have been bound to disarm troops which had taken refuge in her territory. Though she still pretended to be an ally, the line of retreat adopted by the Russians and the Prussians after Bautzen caused Napoleon to suspect the existence of a secret understanding between his father-in-law and his openly avowed enemies. The possibilities which Austria's adherence to the Alliance would open up seem to have so startled Napoleon that he was led into what is generally acknowledged to have been one of the most fatal mistakes he ever made. He halted his armies, arrested the further progress of the campaign, agreed to a truce—to which the Allies were only too glad to consent—and at Prague opened negotiations for peace. This secured the Allies time, and time was what the Allies, and Austria in particular, most desired. Russia wanted it to enable her to bring up the great levies she had raised during the enthusiasm of the previous year. They had now been converted into soldiers, but enormous distances and bad roads separated St. Petersburg, Moscow and the still more distant Russian provinces from Bohemia whose borders had now become the theatre of operations. The time thus gained enabled Prussia to fill the depleted ranks of her army with the efficient, well-drilled soldiers furnished under the Short Service

System, which the genius of Scharnhorst, Gneisenau and Stein had created. It enabled the secret societies, now supported by powerful governments, to sap the very foundations of Napoleon's strength, even in the German States where his word was still law; and last, but not least, it gave the sovereigns who sought his downfall time to obtain from England the subsidies which were so much needed by states impoverished through his wars, his " Continental system," and the exactions of his armies.

Napoleon wished for peace, but the terms he demanded were preposterous, while those offered by Austria were fair and reasonable. He had now retrieved the honour of the French army after its grievous misfortunes of the previous year. His country was weighed down with taxation and drained of its manhood to find soldiers for his wars. He knew she longed for peace, and all his best Marshals impressed upon him the fruitlessness of further hostilities. But his pride would not allow him to make peace upon any but the most exacting terms, which the events, so far, of this campaign did not warrant his demanding. In this, which I deem to have been the turning point in his career, he certainly did not show the great wisdom he displayed upon nearly every other serious occasion in his life. He undoubtedly misunderstood the strength of the forces, of the moral forces especially, with which he had now to contend. His unbounded energy and the great machinery he had inherited from the Revolution as its executor—and in many a sense he was its embodiment also—had hitherto enabled him to make time tell in his favour. It usually does tell in favour of the despot who has to fight against a confederacy of many long-established nations bound by the traditions of their old-fashioned and perhaps cumbersome mode of military procedure. But he was no longer contending against governments which, out of tune with the epoch, were fighting exclusively for the preservation of an archaic state policy as best they could with armies made up of unwilling recruits. He had now to face the rulers of an almost united Europe, each leading a nation even more anxious to destroy him than those rulers were themselves.

If the Allies were sincere in wishing for peace, Napoleon ought to have made it after Bautzen; if they were not so and only wished to deceive him in order to gain time, he ought to have seen through their deceit, and pressing them hard before their reinforcements could arrive, he should have forced them to make peace upon the lines which Austria declared she was willing to negotiate upon.

Hitherto I have said little or nothing of the war which England was then waging against Napoleon in the Peninsula. And yet, when all is said and done and every allowance is made for the stern determination of the Czar and his allies to prosecute the war to the bitter end, it must be generally admitted that it was the war maintained by England against France in Spain by land and all over the world at sea, together with the pressure which she brought to bear upon Napoleon by means of her lavish subsidies, that eventually destroyed him. The "Spanish ulcer," which since 1808 had been tapping the strength of the

French army, now told seriously against Napoleon's power in Germany. The successive defeats sustained by his Marshals beyond the Pyrenees had seriously reduced the number of French troops available for service elsewhere. But, hitherto, Wellington's victories were only of local effect; for the French army in Spain had all along been vastly superior in numbers to his, the only organised force Napoleon had to contend with there. So much was this the case, that it was only the impossibility of any effective union between the French Marshals which enabled Wellington to hold his own—a circumstance to which he was also indebted for being able to defeat them separately one after the other. But in 1813 the case was altogether different. The battle of Vittoria—fought June 21st—was no mere local victory. It was not only a crushing, a final blow to Napoleon's power in Spain, but it laid the south of France open to invasion by Wellington's thoroughly efficient Anglo-Portuguese army at a moment when Austria, Prussia, and Russia were preparing to invade her from the east. Beyond all doubt this great victory of Wellington's had an important influence in determining the action of Austria during the truce and the negotiations at Prague.

When hostilities recommenced on August 11th, the Allied forces in Germany—about 500,000 strong with 1800 guns—were divided into the three following armies: the main army in Bohemia, under Schwarzenberg, of about 320,000; that of Blucher in Silesia of about 95,000; and of Bernadotte, at Berlin, of about 90,000 men. There were also some divisions, about 40,000 in all, employed in watching the French garrisons of Danzig and Hamburg; and behind all, there were reserves of about 250,000 men. This calculation of the Allies' strength does not include the troops in Spain under Wellington or the Austrian forces in Bavaria and Italy.

After all Napoleon's great exertions, he had, available for field operations on and beyond the Elbe, only about 400,000 men with 1200 guns.

The Allies determined upon the following scheme of operations. Bernadotte was to cover Berlin and drive Davoust from Hamburg, and Blucher was to engage the enemy in front whilst Schwarzenberg, with the main army, was to operate against his communications. This last-named move would, it was felt, be greatly facilitated by the configuration of the mountains which form the northern frontier of Bohemia.

Schwarzenberg's army, with which were the Czar, the Emperor of Austria, and the King of Prussia, was to march behind the screen of these mountains and fall upon the defences of the Elbe, attacking Dresden from the south, and, if possible from the west.

Bernadotte's army at Berlin was continually growing in size and increasing in efficiency. Its nucleus consisted of the Swedes he had brought with him from the north, a handful of English, some Russians, and the skeleton of a Prussian army to be completed by reservists and recruits. These Prussians joined in large numbers all eager for what they now felt to be a national war and full both of patriotic enthusiasm and bitter hatred of the French. Bernadotte's army was a ource of considerable anxiety to Napoleon for he felt that if he did not crush it at once, whilst it was still weak from want of organisation, it was bound to become a formidable thorn in his left flank when he advanced beyond the Elbe. Blucher, by his fiery patriotism, imparted to his army in Silesia a weight and consequence far beyond its numbers ; and General York's corps, which formed part of it, also added to its

SCHWARZENBERG.

importance from the fact that it had been in Russia with Napoleon and had been the first to desert him.

But notwithstanding the numerical superiority of the Allies they still dreaded to engage the great king of war himself. Impressed doubtless by their failure in the first phase of the campaign and also by the fact that their rapid retreat both at Lutzen and Bautzen had rendered those French victories almost fruitless in result for Napoleon, they resolved upon a novel method of procedure which they endeavoured to follow for the rest of the war. It was, to attack, whenever they could, any army that was commanded by any of Napoleon's Marshals, but if Napoleon were present, to retreat and avoid a battle. This policy proved fatal to most of Napoleon's projects, for although during the following campaign he made many rapid advances and forced marches in the hope of compelling his enemy to fight, he always failed to do so. Wherever he appeared the threatened Allied commander retired, like an *ignis fatuus*, before him.

It is quite possible that as yet none of the Allied sovereigns may have seriously contemplated Napoleon's forcible deposition, much less have formulated any plan for bringing it about. But it must have been very evident to himself that if his army were defeated, or if he even failed to obtain the great victory between the Elbe and the Oder upon which his hopes were fixed, he would soon find himself standing on French soil in defence of the Rhine frontier. Already Wellington threatened invasion from the south, and Napoleon felt that he could best defend the Pyrenees by a masterstroke, as of yore, in Germany. For this his best chance lay in a vigorous offensive beyond the Elbe over which, after Lutzen, he held all the passages. Its strong places being in his possession made it into a good fortified base pushed forward into Germany from behind which he might deliver his blows in safety. His plan was to operate with three armies: one under Oudinot against Berlin, another under Macdonald against Blucher, whilst, with a large central force under his own immediate command he would be able to rapidly reinforce either of those armies. He would thus temporarily make the reinforced army far superior in numbers to its immediate antagonist. Besides these armies there were the Corps of Vandamme, St. Cyr, Victor, and Poniatowski, who were intended to hold the Elbe and watch Bohemia.

This scheme of campaign may be fairly described as over-ambitious and on too grand a scale when we remember how numerically inferior his army was to the Allied forces arrayed against him. It was a bold game, an enormous venture for the great prize of Universal Empire at which he had aimed so long. In framing it he seems to have ignored the disasters of the previous year, and to have refused to admit that his renown and the fear in which all nations held him were not what they had been before he had led his armies across the Niemen. But in his opinion it was the only safe course to take if he meant to regain his former authority in Europe and to bring back its sovereigns to their previous state of vassalage to himself. A great a startling military success was the first the all-important essential for his plan, and he was as fully sensible of the difficulties to be encountered before he could secure it as he was of the dangers to his throne which the struggle would involve. This policy, which he deliberately adopted, was on a par with the "nothing risk nothing win" the "all or nothing" play of the gambler, who having had a long run of ill luck, and finding himself nearly ruined unwisely and recklessly stakes his all upon one venture

Finding that Blucher was the first of his antagonists

DRESDEN, 1813.

to move, Napoleon opened the campaign by a rapid march to support Macdonald. But before Napoleon could do anything against the veteran Prussian he had fallen back, having ascertained that the Emperor was present with the army in his front.

Just at this same time news reached Napoleon that the main army of the Allies was crossing the Bohemian frontier with the evident intention of attacking Dresden. He at once marched back upon that place, gathering together as he went all his forces from the Bohemian frontier.

St. Cyr had been left to hold Dresden, but its dismantled defences, which Napoleon had ordered to be restored, were still in a very imperfect condition. Napoleon's intention was to cross the Elbe near the Bohemian frontier and whilst St. Cyr held the Allied Army in front to fall upon its rear, and, cutting it off from every line of retreat, to utterly destroy it. A grand combination worthy of the great genius who framed it. But St. Cyr sent him an urgent despatch to say he could not undertake to defend Dresden as it was then. Another plan was therefore necessary and it was formed on the instant. He ordered Vandamme with 30,000 men to occupy a position in the gorges of the Erzgebirge on the Allied line ot retreat, and moved himself upon Dresden with the remainder of the troops at his disposal. He reached that city at 10 A.M. on August 26th, his headquarters having marched about 120 miles in four days. His troops, though fatigued—for the roads were very bad from heavy rain—pressed eagerly forward, as in their best days, to meet the enemy.

The operations which led to the battles round Dresden are most instructive for the military student. On one side—until Vandamme's defeat at Kulm—the ablest strategy, the most fearless decision, the clearest grasp of the position, and the most rapid movements; on the other, divided counsels, feeble indecision, and a dread of facing their redoubtable adversary. The presence with the Allied Army of Emperors, Kings, and their attendant ministers and advisers so delayed its movements that it was not until late in the afternoon of August 26th that the Allies began their attack upon Dresden, being then under the belief that Napoleon was absent. For so much did his presence count on any field of battle that as soon as they discovered their mistake orders were at once issued to suspend the attack. It was nevertheless made—in sheer helplessness it would seem—and was bloodily repulsed.

By the following day, August 27th, all the available French troops had arrived in front of the Allied Army. Napoleon made a careful reconnaissance of the position it occupied covering the heights round Dresden on the left bank of the Elbe. The centre was crowded with masses of men but the left was isolated beyond the deep ravine through which the Weisseritz flows into that river below the city. Upon this left Napoleon resolved to deliver his chief attack whilst he held in check the densely-occupied centre by the fire of a great array of field-guns. His attack upon the Allied left was most successful; and, as soon as their infantry had been driven from the villages they occupied into the open Murat, who directed the operation, poured down his horsemen upon it. This isolated left wing was utterly destroyed and the Allied Army was cut off from all hope of retreat by the roads in rear of that flank. In the meantime Ney, who had operated against the Allied right, succeeded in cutting off their retreat by that flank, and their crowded centre had suffered heavily from the batteries which Napoleon had massed against it.

Like Turenne's battle at Entzheim, these operations round Dresden were executed under a heavy downpour of rain, which destroyed the roads and so rendered all retreat most difficult.

This was the only occasion upon which Napoleon ever attacked both wings of a superior enemy in position contenting himself simply with a heavy artillery fire upon the hostile centre. The object he here aimed at was to cut off the Allies from their easiest line of retreat and compel them to retire by their centre upon the passes through the Erzgebirge in which Vandamme was posted to bar the way.

Obliged to fall back, principally from want of provisions and ammunition the arrival of which had been prevented by the badness of the roads, the Allies thus found themselves restricted to one road as their line of retreat. At first Napoleon pressed their retiring columns with his wonted energy and as long as he remained to direct the operations everything went well. Knowing the position which Vandamme occupied in the mountains he was justified in believing that the destruction of the whole Allied Army was certain. The capture of the two Emperors and the King of Prussia would most probably re-establish his renown and authority which had been so seriously shaken by the disastrous retreat from Moscow. How all these speculations, these hopes, must have filled Napoleon's mind at this critical moment! How he must have congratulated himself upon having adopted the audacious policy he had followed instead of standing upon the defensive near the Rhine, as most leaders would have done under similar circumstances! What stupendous anxieties must then have crowded that mighty brain! What consequences, not only for himself but for all Europe, depended upon the turn which the events of the next few hours might take! Oh, war is a terrible thing from every aspect; but in none is it more so than in its awe-inspiring uncertainty, and the chances which affect its results. Well indeed may Turenne have said, that after the ablest combinations have been planned by the first generals three-fourths of the result still depend upon accident. Here is an illustration in point, for here once more the evil genius of what I may call Napoleon's declining years snatched from him the results which he had every right to expect from his recent victory.

He suddenly relinquished his personal direction of the pursuit and went back to Dresden. That it was illness or physical prostration which caused him to do so there can be, I think, no doubt. The man who hitherto throughout this campaign had been on horseback at daybreak each morning when there was fighting to be expected was not likely to have abandoned this pursuit—upon which his very existence as Emperor depended—had he been strong enough, bodily and mentally, to have continued it. But at this critical moment he seems to have suddenly become an altered man. We know that he was exposed during the battle to the drenching rain which fell that day and this may have brought on an attack of that mysterious malady to which I referred in the previous chapter. This is borne out by the fact that there is a sudden and unmistakable change in the tone and spirit of the letters he wrote after his return to Dresden from those he had previously written. At first his orders for the pursuit are clear, vigorous, and characteristic. Suddenly the Marshals are left without instructions and the pursuit is relaxed in consequence.

The Allies, no longer harassed or pressed in rear, had time thus allowed them to realise that with their overwhelming numbers they could easily brush Vandamme from their path. This they did at Kulm on August 30th, his cavalry and about ten thousand foot alone escaping to rejoin Napoleon. Vandamme, who boasted that he feared neither God nor devil, was taken prisoner and all his guns and the rest of his force were either captured or destroyed. "Vandamme," said Napoleon, "is very precious to me for if ever I have occasion to make war against the infernal regions he is the only general I have who would be capable of tackling the devil."

In the meantime Oudinot with 60,000 men had been heavily defeated on August 26th at Gross Beeren by Bernadotte with an army over 150,000 strong and composed of better elements than Napoleon had given it credit for. Gérard's Division, which had hastened to Oudinot's assistance, was almost entirely destroyed. This was Napoleon's first experience of the power

F

which a Short Service System, well applied, gives the ruler who is shrewd enough to make use of it. Though Swedes, English, and Russians were important elements in Bernadotte's army at Berlin it was on Bulow's Prussian Corps, formed almost entirely of Reservists, that most of the fighting at Gross Beeren had fallen.

On August 26th Macdonald's army, about 80,000 strong, having been caught by Blucher in the act of passing the Katzbach was driven back upon its swollen torrent and escaped with barely 20,000 men.

These defeats at Kulm, Gross Beeren, and the Katzbach were heavy blows to the fighting efficiency of Napoleon's army in Germany, and were deadly wounds to his reputation for invincibility. They were all the more serious because they served, in a remarkable degree, to give new life to the Allied forces whose spirit had been damped by their defeats at Dresden and by the perils of their retreat from that city—perils which were appalling as long as Napoleon was able to direct the pursuit in person. They inspired all Germans with increased determination to fight the war out to the bitter end, and increased both the number of recruits who joined the regular army and of the Corps of Free Lances who now harassed Napoleon's communications everywhere. Time was working against him and every hour that did not represent progress for his arms was a fatal loss to him; for England was now straining every nerve to re-arm the populations whom, after his early career of victory, he had disarmed lest they should fight against him.

Napoleon now despatched Ney with fresh troops

towards Berlin. He had intended to reinforce him with his own central army but the necessity of supporting Macdonald's broken army obliged him instead to hurry forward against Blucher. That fighting Field Marshal, however, as soon as he heard that Napoleon was with the army marching to attack him, fell back promptly to avoid a battle. Meantime the Grand Army of the Allies, relieved of Napoleon's presence, again passed the Bohemian mountains to threaten Dresden for the second time. This move brought back Napoleon in a hurry to that city in the hope of once more catching that Army, and in this instance of destroying it after he had beaten it in battle. Here again he was doomed to disappointment for as soon as his return became known the Allies again retired behind the Erzgebirge, and Blucher resumed the offensive against Macdonald. Meanwhile, Ney, unsupported and left without the personal direction of Napoleon, had advanced against Bernadotte and was severely defeated at Dennewitz on September 6th.

All Napoleon's movements were closely watched by irregular troops who obtained the best information everywhere from the inhabitants who in all districts were well-wishing informers and self-constituted spies. On the other hand, he had the utmost difficulty in obtaining reliable information about his enemies' doings or whereabouts. Nothing was more remarkable about Napoleon's personal conduct of a war than the skill and energy he always displayed in his arrangements for securing, at every phase of a campaign, the earliest and best intelligence of all that was taking place in the theatre of war whilst he carefully concealed his own movements and intentions from the enemy. He lays it down as a maxim that the general who has to remain in ignorance of his enemies' proceedings is ignorant of his trade. Yet in this campaign, especially after the truce, he could learn very little about the distribution and strength of the Allied Armies opposed to him; whilst on the other hand, although the efforts made and the methods pursued by Schwarzenberg and the Allied headquarters for this purpose were feeble in the extreme, they had good information about the French armies. The passionate hatred of millions which his "Continental system" and his soldiers' treatment of the inhabitants had roused against him made it difficult for his spies to act, and this in a great measure made up for the deficiencies of the Allied leaders in this respect. His complete ignorance of the strength and real composition of Bernadotte's army in Berlin, which was the main cause of Ney's and Oudinot's disastrous defeats, is a good illustration of what I mean. But the general failure of his Marshals in 1813 was largely owing to the military system which he had created, I mean the centralization of all initiative in himself.

Napoleon's armies were thus rapidly crumbling away under the hands of his Marshals whilst the Allies successfully evaded his own blows. He made repeated efforts to overwhelm Blucher but to no purpose, for as I have stated that wily soldier either retreated or by calling in his detached forces became too strong to be attacked with any certainty of success. Upon each occasion Napoleon was compelled to relinquish the hope of crushing Blucher and to fall back nearer France.

These retirements of their great adversary in person increased the confidence of the Allies. Bennigsen, with a fresh Russian army, was near at hand, and this, amongst other reasons, now caused the Allied leaders to resolve upon taking the offensive. Their plan was, that Blucher and Bernadotte on one flank and the main army, strengthened by Bennigsen, on the other were to cross the Elbe and join hands in rear of Napoleon's army, and so cut it off from its base on the Rhine. But before this could be accomplished the defection of Bavaria rendered Napoleon's forward position so dangerous that he felt obliged to fall back upon Leipzig with all his forces, a point so central for all lines of communication between France and Germany that he could not afford to allow the Allies to seize it.

In this historic neighbourhood both the contending sides now gathered for a great battle. It began on October 16th and lasted three days. Upon each of these days the Allies received such large reinforcements that they were able to hem in Napoleon closer and closer within a circle so narrow that at last he could manœuvre no longer. At every point around him he was met with greatly superior numbers. On the 18th, in the middle of the battle, the Saxon and Würtemberg contingents went over to the Allies and actually turned their weapons against their friends of the morning.

Napoleon's chief of the staff, accustomed always to

victory when carrying out the schemes of his great master, had made no proper provision for the retreat which now became inevitable. No extra bridges had been laid across the Elster and none of the impedimenta had been sent to the rear. When, therefore, the retreat began in the early morning of October 19th, there was great confusion from the intermingling of troops and baggage. The rearguard fought splendidly but was eventually cut off and either captured or destroyed through the premature destruction of the bridge it was to have retreated by. This battle cost Napoleon about 50,000 men, 300 guns, and a great mass of military material; but yet when his old allies, the Bavarians, strove to bar his passage he brushed them aside with ease and succeeded in recrossing the Rhine at Mayence on November 2nd. Not more, however, than about 75,000 or 80,000 good troops, the remains of the large army with which he opened the campaign six months before, crossed that river with him.

The Allies, instead of pursuing vigorously, spent the next two months—almost uselessly—in reducing the many fortresses still held by the French on the Elbe the Oder and the Vistula. Had they pressed Napoleon hard they might have destroyed his army before it could recross the Rhine. Had this been the result of the campaign the Allied sovereigns might have eaten their Christmas dinner in the Tuileries, and we should not have had the history of the interesting but useless campaign of 1814 to record. But the weakness and folly of the Allies in failing to pursue with all their might not only gave some respite to

Napoleon's jaded troops, but also gave him time to prepare for that most remarkable campaign which began about the end of the following January.

Both in 1812 and 1813 the collapse of the Imperial power was mainly due to causes which for some years had been sapping the foundations on which it rested, whilst they left the edifice itself, apparently, as stately and imposing as ever. The failure of Schwarzenberg's Austrians in 1812 and the defection of York were only more overt signs of what was happening in detail wherever Napoleon's armies moved or wherever the authority of his edicts was recognised. The sentiment of all European nations was bitterly hostile to him, and this accounts largely for the slow movement and frequent destruction of the supply-trains upon which his army depended. The drivers and conductors—mostly German—forced to serve with these trains, loathed helping their conqueror.

The composition of his army, more than any other one cause, had forced him onwards when he hesitated at Smolensk as to whether he should winter there or push on for Moscow. The great forces with which he appeared in Russia and with which he reappeared in the 1813 campaign were largely swollen by allies held to him only by a belief in his power—in what the world conceived to be his omnipotence. But when that belief was rudely shaken by the destruction of his army in Russia they were only too ready to desert him: in fact, they began to fear his enemies more than they feared him; and in the campaign of 1813 all these hostile elements made themselves more felt than in the previous year.

Independently of Napoleon's failure to destroy his enemy after the battle of Dresden he made several mistakes this year. But they were more mistakes in diplomacy than in the practice of war. His rejection of the terms proposed by Austria during the truce will always seem the height of folly to most men; and, amongst the errors in his military plans we are most struck with his having locked up, to no useful purpose, an army of about a hundred and fifty thousand soldiers in the fortresses on the Oder and the Vistula. It is easy to pick holes in the character even of a saint, to point out errors made by even the real kings of men in their management of public affairs. But the more closely we study the proceedings of Napoleon in 1813, notwithstanding the mistakes he made, the greater appears his remarkable individuality, and the more inclined we are to say with the Duke of Wellington about him, " How much the fate of the world depends upon the temper and passions of one man!"

As I have said of his campaign in Russia I say of this in Germany, Napoleon in 1813 was not the man he was in 1796 or in 1805. His conceptions were as great, the grandeur of his undertakings was as striking, but his execution was not as of yore. His career of brilliant success had made him believe that he was not only different from other men in brain-power but that a special goddess of victory was his guardian angel, and that he was the favoured son of Fortune. The plans he devised entitled him to expect success and he seems to have believed that a special providence—his "star"—would preside over their execution. Although this was apparently never absent from his mind yet no man ever left the execution of his plans less to chance than he did as long as his health and strength were normal. In this campaign we read of him being on horseback at all hours watching the enemy and reconnoitring the position for himself, personally superintending the passage of his troops and trains over rivers, and doing all that any commander in his best days could have done to avoid failure. But over and over again we find luck run against him.

In the war-game we now play so generally in our garrison towns the dice have to be thrown in certain cases when squadrons of equal strength charge one another. Men sometimes say that, as war is a science, the introduction of this element of chance into the game robs it of much of its instructional value. But those who know what real war is smile at this criticism. They know that an accidental pain in the stomach or a clod in the eye of either leader at the critical moment just before a charge may always decide the result. The accidents which influence that result in real war render it often quite as much a matter of chance as in the throw of the dice in the Kriegspiel of peace.

As far as any one now can judge of what might what ought to have happened after the battle of Dresden, it seems very evident to me that had not Napoleon withdrawn, as he did, from the personal direction of the pursuit nothing could have saved the Allied Army from destruction or capitulation. I can only find one explanation of that withdrawal, and it is the sudden collapse through illness at the moment of Napoleon's mental and physical powers. The ball was at his foot; but he turned back instead of making a goal and his subordinates could not make it for him.

# CHAPTER III.

## THE CAMPAIGN OF 1814.

DURING the month of November 1813, the French armies, after their defeat at Leipzig, were driven helter-skelter towards the Rhine, and the Allies in their wake approached that river on their way to Paris. When the Allied sovereigns reached Frankfort, the difficulties of their great task seem to have impressed them, for they began to realise how unequal their generals were to cope with Napoleon. It is therefore scarcely to be wondered at that, notwithstanding their recent successes, they were still prepared to treat with him on terms that would have left him as sovereign over a greater France than any of its legitimate kings had ever ruled over. Besides, his father-in-law, the Emperor of Austria, had not yet resolved to dethrone his own daughter. They offered him as frontiers the Pyrenees, Switzerland and the Rhine to the sea, besides giving him Nice and Savoy. These were the boundaries which had been the day-dream of Lewis XIV. and which Marlborough's victories had alone prevented him from securing.

When 1814 opened, Napoleon's position was critical. With the exception of the fortresses which he still unwisely held on the Oder the Vistula and elsewhere he had lost the whole of Germany. All the great military powers had become—one after the other—his enemies, and their armies were in full march for Paris. Italy and Switzerland had just turned against him; the English fleets had driven his flag off the ocean, and Wellington, at the head of a thoroughly organised army well experienced in war and flushed with recent victories, was already on French soil threatening his capital from the south.

How seriously the defeats experienced at Moscow and Leipzig had wounded France no man knew better than Napoleon. But in the game of war, especially when a despot like Lewis XIV. is pitted against a Confederation of many nations, time often brings many chances to the weaker side. He trusted so much to this and to his own skill that, although he knew that every arithmetical calculation was against him he deliberately preferred to trust his luck and expose his country to the likelihood of a mortal blow rather than accept any terms which should injure his own future renown as a ruler and a conqueror. To satisfy his craving for immortal fame the fair fields of France must be given over to the ravages of infuriated Cossacks and her capital occupied by revengeful Prussians.

The France he had to work upon was, however, no longer the France of 1805. The fields were largely fallow from the lack of men and horses to till them, and nearly all agricultural work had devolved upon the women and children. After a quarter of a century of revolutionary horrors and imperial victories exhausted France cried aloud for peace at any price; but her despot would not hearken. He would not have it at the cost of his own glory and future fame, and for this cruel decision future ages will condemn him. Come what might he was determined to immortalise his name by the display of what his great military genius could do under the most adverse circumstances. He would have it remembered by all generations of Frenchmen that he had not despaired of the destinies and fortune of France even in her darkest hour. Under a pretended all-absorbing love for her he hoped to hide the burning craze for fame and immortal renown which now filled his thoughts and which filled them from boyhood to his death. He kept for his brother's ear alone that according to his views of this world, "it is better to die a king than to live as a prince."

In ancient history we read of men who lived almost exclusively for fame, for the admiration of future generations. They cared little for the hardships and the pains of war or how others suffered from them as long as they might hope thereby to render their names immortal. But in this thirst for the applause and worship of peoples yet unborn few have equalled none have exceeded Napoleon. He had entered public life at a time when those around him daily ransacked the histories of Greece and Rome for tales of national heroism, when even the unlettered crowd had learnt to babble of Cæsar and of Brutus. In his early days the names of Leonidas, Epaminondas, Fabricius, Hannibal, Scipio and other Grecian and Roman heroes were constantly on the lips of the real as well as the sham actors in what were then the appalling tragedies of every-day life. Immortal renown was the great aim of Napoleon and no man at any period ever achieved it to a greater degree. No man ever lived more for the future than he did. Very early in his career he felt that historians would class him with Cyrus, Alexander, Mahomet, and the greatest conquerors who had overrun the earth. He knew that his reign would be compared with that of Charlemagne, Henri IV. and Lewis XIV. and his ambition was to leave behind him a name greater than theirs. Were he now to make peace on the Allies' conditions how could he meet on equal terms the spirits of other great conquerors in those Elysian fields of which he loved to talk?

His mind was of that peculiarly superstitious nature that, whilst we may assume he had never bent a knee in true reverence to his Maker, he did firmly believe in some good spirit who watched over him and ensured him success. This guardian angel had pulled him through many great difficulties, more than once even converting defeat into victory. Why should Fortune now turn her back upon the ablest soldier of the age, the wisest and greatest man alive! His thoughts were more occupied with future history and as to how posterity would regard him, than with the present and the events taking place around him. Peering afar off into future ages it would seem as if the glare dazzled his eyes, so that he had no power to take in any exact estimate of the things near and immediately surrounding him. As a soldier he had equalled the fame of Turenne, even of Marlborough; as a king he had brought France greater renown than Lewis XIV.; but he would not, like that monarch, self-styled "the Great," sign away all his glory in any second treaty of Utrecht.

Throughout this campaign Napoleon did all he could to give to his operations the colour of a national war waged, as in 1792, in defence of France against invaders bent upon her destruction. He did his best to pose as a national hero,—he was an inimitable actor,—and when we read in the French histories of the Allied hosts drawn from all points of the compass who were then converging upon Paris, we are apt to think of him as the soldier-patriot, disputing every inch of French territory; as the giant driven to bay, with his back to the wall, dealing out knock-me-down blows first to one then to the other of his antagonists as each in turn dared to assail him. The mind naturally recurs to young William of Nassau's heroic defence of Holland when it was invaded by Lewis XIV. We remember William's splendid patriotism during that prolonged struggle: how he fought almost against hope; how at last, sooner than surrender his country to the invader, he gave back to the sea whole provinces which his industrious countrymen had reclaimed from the Northern Ocean; and how, when tempted by the French king with offers of personal sovereignty, he said he would die in the last ditch sooner than forsake the people who had trusted him. But our William III. loved Holland, the land of his birth, with all his heart with all his soul, he was a real patriot and hero. But superhuman as I believe

Napoleon's genius to have been I cannot feel that in the three last years of his wars he either proved himself a hero or a true French patriot. Had he loved his own personal renown less and France more how different would have been his end! how much useless loss of life how much misery and defeat he would have spared France! When we think of all this, I can well understand the Frenchmen who, loathing his memory, remind us that when, as a youth, he was talking of his future to his most intimate school friend, he said: "I will do these Frenchmen all the harm I can."

Upon his return to Paris after Leipzig he called, as usual, for large levies, but few except mere boys answered the call. He could not find horses for his cavalry and many of the newly-enrolled foot had neither muskets nor belts. Most of the National Guard were in sabots and blouses. He wanted money but time was still more required, and to gain it he strove to obtain an armistice early in the campaign. The Allies would not listen to the proposal. They would make peace at once on their own terms, but would not halt, even to make it, until they had reached Paris. Napoleon never trusted to his luck more than in 1814, feeling that in the very vastness of the combination against him there were many elements that might at any moment declare in his favour. He thoroughly understood the inherent weakness of all Coalitions : on this point, as on many others, he had not studied Marlborough's campaigns in vain. He very naturally looked for the chances which would be afforded him by an Allied Army commanded by three sovereigns, all more or less jealous of one another and each with special interests to serve.

The nine weeks' campaign of 1814 was the only defensive one Napoleon ever waged. In his previous wars he had always taken the initiative and assuming

LANNES.

a vigorous and rapid offensive had overwhelmed his enemy, not only by superior strategy but by the force and rapidity of his blows, until his adversary lay prostrate before him bleeding from every pore.

By November 1st, having placed the Rhine between

his disorganised troops and the enemy, his first idea was to hold that river if possible in order to retain the provinces on its left bank as a recruiting ground and to obtain a revenue from them. He had not expected that the Allies would have embarked in a winter campaign and had fondly hoped that, protected by that river, he would have had time allowed him to reorganise his army and, by the augmentation of another conscription, to prepare it for a new campaign in the following spring. But here his calculations were at fault. His energy was as fierce as ever and his plans and arrangements were stamped with all his usual ability; the Allies moved slowly and timidly and ignorantly after they had crossed the Rhine; he won what he announced in Paris as victories; but notwithstanding all this he never was given the time he required to drill or arm and equip the conscripts who obeyed the Senate's call for 300,000 fresh soldiers. Most people now agree in thinking that as soon as he found the Allies were actually crossing into France, he should have made peace upon the best terms he could obtain.

Many ambitious self-seekers mistake their own personal aims and their mad quest after personal fame for the good and the renown of their country,—this is not uncommon in political life. But Napoleon was far too shrewd and able a man to entertain any such illusion, although he had at all times striven to impress France with the conviction that whatever he did was done purely in her interests, and in 1814 that he was only fighting in her cause. When a prisoner at St. Helena he mendaciously strove to make the world accept this explanation of his strange and reckless conduct in that year.

Determined to carry on the war, as soon as the Allies began to cross the Rhine he felt that with his weakened forces it was hopeless to think of maintaining himself on that river. He accordingly ordered the corps under Ney, Victor, and Marmont, to fall back upon Verdun, Chalons, and Bar-sur-Aube, before the advancing enemy. Besides these there were also available MacDonald's corps and the guard under Mortier and Oudinot. In this year's war the number of troops engaged is more than usually uncertain; besides, Napoleon's very rapid movements and the great exposure to which his men were subjected thinned his ranks day by day. In all wars forced marches and constant movement soon cause the strength of battalions to dwindle away even in fine weather; but the cold and rain of winter and the irregularity of supplies which repeated forced marches entail increase the rate of diminution enormously. The whole of his drilled and equipped army at the date when the Allies passed the Rhine was only something between seventy and eighty thousand, of which about one-fourth were cavalry: the proportion of his guns to men was much larger than was usual at that period. During the progress of the campaign he frequently received reinforcements which materially increased his strength; those which joined the Allies were more numerous, but they brought with them much sickness contracted during their long line of march.

Though Napoleon recovered fairly well from the

disasters of Moscow he never did so from the defeat at Leipzig. For the campaign of 1813 he had still untouched in the vaults of the Tuileries an immense reserve fund upon which to draw when money grew scarce, and the manhood of the country had not been as yet exhausted. This was all changed now and the taxes had become enormous: that on income alone was 25 per cent. for all non-military people. This caused the rich and the middle classes to long for a Bourbon restoration and reduced the poor to abject want. But these taxes came in slowly, and Napoleon soon spent all the ready money which remained to him in refitting his retreating army and in the equipment of the new levies he was collecting. France had no longer her former faith in him and began at last to regard his wars as both endless and aimless. The strictly enforced conscriptions of the last two years had denuded the land of young men: the only males to be seen in the villages were the boys and old fathers of families. In fact, he had forestalled the annual contingents of recruits by some years. In every department of the Empire there was now a decided inclination to resist the conscription as far as men could safely venture to do so. In many districts those drawn to be soldiers had taken to the woods. The worst features of the press-gang in its most oppressive days were distanced by the cruelties of Napoleon's latest conscriptions. Of the 300,000 men voted to reinforce his army after the disasters of Leipzig, only 63,000 had answered the call by January 31st, 1814. The unwisdom and inexpediency of his "Continental system" was now openly acknowledged and freely spoken of, and, amongst what we may at least by courtesy style the ruling classes under such a ruler, there had grown up a craving for that tranquil prosperity which as was now generally believed his wars made impossible. The shocks caused by his recent disasters seemed at last to have aroused France from the state of intoxication into which the dazzling glory of his former victories had sunk her. The Royalists the Republicans the Priest-party as well as the scheming politicians of the Talleyrand type, all were now encouraged by the aspect of affairs within the very borders of France to intrigue against Napoleon and his oppressive rule. The Legislative Body, his faithful slaves as long as he was victorious, now plucked up courage to ask for guarantees for popular liberty and even ventured to restrict his demands for money. He dismissed them in anger; the Senate, still in awe of him, gave him all he wanted. But this summary dismissal of the Legislature tended to reduce his influence and his power to obtain from a discouraged, as well as an impoverished people, the men and supplies he then so urgently needed. Indeed, such became the state of public feeling that he did not dare to render that popular force, the National Guard, as really effective as he might have done.

Napoleon's aims were still directed to great objects, as if he had met with no crushing disasters during the two previous years; his schemes were still so vast, so far-reaching, that he would not bring down his thoughts to so restricted a compass as the mere defence of France. Bent on great plans for future action, he had in 1812–13 left a considerable army behind him in the fortresses of Germany which employed on the Elbe in 1813 might have insured him victory. In the same way he could not now make up his mind to concentrate all his resources for the defensive campaign which he clearly saw was then before him. The thirty or forty thousand seasoned troops with which Suchet held Catalonia would have been an invaluable addition to his small army in the plains of Champagne; Eugène was operating in Italy with an army of about the same strength; Augereau at Lyons was organising a new force; and Soult might have spared some valuable troops, had Napoleon ordered him to restrict his army to purely defensive operations against Wellington. As in the previous year's campaign, Napoleon's general plan of operations was too ambitious and was not in scale with the actual position in which he then found himself.

In judging of Napoleon's decision to hold on as long as he could to the largest possible extent of territory, both in 1813 and the following year, we must not, however, forget that he was fighting for recruiting areas. Wherever there were enough French troops to maintain his authority he was able to raise soldiers, for he still had zealous friends in every province; but as soon as his authority was no longer recognised the countries so lost to him too often became a valuable recruiting ground for his enemies. For example, when the Confederation of the Rhine had been broken up as the result of his recent misfortunes, nearly 150,000 troops that had previously fought under his banner were transferred to swell the armies opposed to him. The countries which had formed that Confederation, being nearest to France,

FREDERICK WILLIAM III. OF PRUSSIA.

were of all others then the most important on that account.

Some of Napoleon's best troops had come from Piedmont and Tuscany—in fact Eugène's army was almost entirely recruited in Italy—but at the same time to have brought them into France might have entailed their loss through desertion to the enemy, as had happened in the cases of Saxony, Wurtemberg and Bavaria when Napoleon evacuated those kingdoms. Besides he counted on Eugène's army, aided by Augereau, to secure the alliance and assistance of the Swiss amongst whom Napoleon had many ardent friends. It was his intention that Eugène, thus supported, should fall upon the Allies' lines of communication after their armies had entered France, and he hoped that the warlike inhabitants of Alsace and Lorraine would be thus encouraged to act with greater vigour in the enemy's rear. As a matter of fact those two provinces did strenuously oppose the advance of the Allies. With the exception of Augereau's comparatively small army, Napoleon could hardly count upon assistance from any of these sources if he restricted his plan of operation to the fields watered by the Marne and the Seine, where it was evident he must fight to protect Paris. But on the other hand if Eugène's army joined him, the Emperor of Austria would be able to move his troops under Bellegarde from Italy into France.

The case of his armies in Spain was different. It is difficult not to think that Napoleon was indulging in expectations there which the battle of Vittoria had made unworthy of serious consideration. Time pressed, and as soon as he found that the Allies meant to cross the Rhine he should have sent back Ferdinand to Madrid; but instead of doing this, we find him at the eleventh hour negotiating terms for that king's restoration. His reason for this was, that by keeping up the army under Soult to a respectable figure and by retaining possession of Catalonia with the army of Suchet, he hoped to so arrange matters with Spain that, under the returned monarch, Wellington's position would be rendered politically impossible. Were he relieved of all pressure from that quarter by this withdrawal of the English from Spain, he might be able to rally to him the armies of both Soult and Suchet.

But Wellington's complete victory at Vittoria had stamped these schemes with the ominous words, "too late." Suchet's hold upon Catalonia had become little more than an isolated and irrelevant detail which, if persisted in, could only involve the ultimate loss of the French garrisons stationed in that province; and Soult's army, though admirably led, was unable to withstand Wellington's triumphant invasion of France. It is dangerous, indeed presumptuous, for any soldier to criticise Napoleon's military conceptions and plans; but it strikes military students of this campaign that he would have done better had he restricted Soult's army to gaining time by an active defensive on the Pyrenean frontier and ordered every French soldier that could be spared from it and from Spain generally to join his army in the valleys of the Marne and the Seine.

As long as the French arms were victorious in Central Europe the elements of opposition to his authority were apparently feeble and were easily suppressed wherever they showed themselves; but as soon as the ebbing tide of failure set in and that Napoleon's star was seen to be undoubtedly on the wane the decline of his power proceeded with an increasing rapidity until the final crash came. The vast French Empire of 1811 provided him with immense resources in men. He commanded the services of Poles, Italians, Swiss, Saxons, Danes, Wurtembergers, and Bavarians, and he was able to extract money and material from others who were not friendly to him. As his dominion, however, became reduced in extent by every step he took backwards not only were these supplies cut off but the larger became the armies opposed to him. The zealous self-sacrifice of whole nations, supported by the inexhaustible wealth of England, brought successively into the field masses of men who eventually swept away his power as if by an ever-increasing avalanche pouring down upon the collapsing structure of his Empire.

There is yet another excuse for Napoleon's determination to fight rather than make peace in 1814. Before the Allies crossed the Rhine he had calculated that they would make large detachments for the purpose of besieging the fortresses in which he had left garrisons behind. He also thought they would require armies for various duties in the provinces now being restored to their legitimate rulers. He did not, consequently, anticipate so large a disproportion between his own army and that of the Allies when both had taken the field in France. But before crossing the Rhine the Allies had almost exclusively employed their militia to invest or besiege the French garrisons in Germany; and in their advance from that river towards Paris they stopped to besiege no fortress, contenting themselves with observing or investing them. This was what Malborough intended to do when, early in his wars, he urged the Dutch to allow him to march direct upon Paris and there dictate terms to Lewis XIV.

I have thus dwelt upon the larger features of the war in 1814 because I think it is misleading to the student of history to direct his attention exclusively to the operations in the valleys of the Marne and the Seine. I am glad to find that of late years there has been a natural tendency, amongst those who carefully follow all the events in Napoleon's career, to revolt against any isolated treatment of this campaign as a kind of academic study upon the influence on defensive operations of two lines of river in a theatre of war. The able summary of this campaign by Sir E. Hamley and the manner in which he has treated its remarkable events has long tended, in my opinion to unduly concentrate attention upon the movements of the Allies and of Napoleon between the Marne and the Seine to the exclusion of all the other influences which helped to bring about the abdication of the great soldier-Emperor. In almost every campaign the questions which determine a general in his decisions are of a much wider scope than the mere strategical or tactical movements which can be executed along certain features of a particular line of country. But, at any rate, "the decline and fall of Napoleon" cannot be well understood unless we fully realise the basis upon which his power and supremacy rested and how seriously that foundation had been already shaken before the Allies crossed the Rhine.

No technical criticism of his magnificent strategy, no mere professional analysis of his splendid tactics on the field of battle will suffice.

By the end of 1813 there were about a million of men under arms for the avowed object of pulling down Napoleon from his position as Dictator in Europe; but we must study the moral as well as the physical forces that worked against him if we would fully comprehend his fall. Throughout the greater part of Europe there were two parties then, one favourable, the other bitterly hostile to him. The first was still under the influence of the enormous advantages they had gained through the French Revolution and from the success of its armies; the second was smarting under the pressure of Napoleon's Continental System and the remembrance of the many injuries and insults received from his soldiers. Time and the shortness of human memory for favours received had acted against the party friendly to him, and every day strengthened that which hated him. The agencies which Captain Mahan has so ably traced in his interesting work on the influence of sea-power were also at work against him; but there were others also. The spoliation of Italy and Switzerland, the gradual springing up in all the provinces of ancient Germany of a common German feeling bitterly hostile to France, and the social reforms introduced into Prussia by the able statesmanship of Stein, were amongst the chief causes which acted powerfully in developing a determined opposition to Napoleon's supremacy.

The Allies built a golden bridge for his retreat over

the Rhine as their pursuit after Leipzig was feeble in the extreme. They did not begin to cross that river until December 21st, 1813, having reached it in three columns: one had marched upon the Lower Rhine through Holland sweeping, as it passed, that nation into the coalition against Napoleon; another under Blucher, about 50,000 strong, upon the Middle Rhine at Coblentz; and the third and largest, about 120,000 men under Schwarzenberg, upon Bâle where it crossed by the stone bridge. Bâle belonged to Switzerland, which threw in its lot with the Coalition. Before the end of the year the two last-named armies were assembled in the valleys of the Marne and the Seine. They were no longer prepared to grant Napoleon the favourable terms they had proposed at Frankfort, for they had begun to realise that there could be no permanent tranquillity in Europe as long as he was left to rule France upon any conditions.

Before passing the Rhine the Allies issued a manifesto to the French people declaring that it was their wish to see France strong and prosperous. They endeavoured to impress upon all classes that it was Napoleon alone who stood between them and the peace which was so ardently longed for. Their "only conquest," they said, "should be peace—a peace that should give permanent repose to France and to all Europe." Following the example of the old Directory, they declared they did not make war upon the people but upon their rulers. The Allied armies were generally received with cordiality as friends come to give them back peace. To the shame, however, of the invaders, they sullied their operations by great excesses; but when we remember how all grades in the French army had pillaged and oppressed the inhabitants of Central Europe it is not to be wondered at that, having in their turn become conquerors, they should take vengeance for the wrongs and insults they had previously endured.

Napoleon now found himself under the unlooked-for necessity of having to defend his capital against the Allies who were marching upon it. Amongst the unfavourable conditions under which he was compelled to begin this struggle, the retired position of his fortresses behind the Rhine frontier was a serious misfortune. Hitherto his war policy had always been to dictate terms to his enemies in *their* capitals, and the result of his far-reaching conquests was that he had neglected the girdle of fortresses with which Lewis XIV. had protected the eastern frontier of his kingdom. But that frontier had been left behind: it was not Napoleon's frontier and he had consequently thought it useless to spend money upon the maintenance of works designed to defend the bygone limits of a restricted France. These fortresses were not, therefore, in a state to resist any siege. Besides, typhus fever, too often the scourge of a defeated army, was decimating his troops in those places, having been imported from Russia and by the garrisons lately withdrawn from Germany.

Napoleon saw the net that was being drawn around him by the mighty hosts which now threatened Paris from all points. But he was not without hope, for he could foresee in the coming struggle numerous possibilities for the exercise of his commanding ability;

and one of the most striking peculiarities of his declining fortunes was, that like the ruined speculator he based his calcalutions more upon the possible than the probable. He believed that his army in the Pyrenees, under the skilful leadership of Soult, would suffice to keep Wellington at a distance long enough to enable him to dispose of his own immediate antagonists. He calculated much upon the national spirit which the invasion of France would call forth; and although it was not as strong or as pronounced as he had anticipated, it is most creditable to the oppressed and ruined people that it did show itself, especially in some districts. He believed this feeling would animate his soldiers, and inspire them with a dash and valour even greater than ever. His was an army of Frenchmen fighting to defend the soil of France: what might he not therefore expect from them under his superlatively able leadership? Opposed to him were the armies of three nations and many principalities, each with its special aims and jealousies. One was the army of his father-in-law who was present with it and would not surely allow his daughter to be deposed or her husband driven into exile. No one knew better than he did the weakness of a divided command, especially when the commanders were like those now pursuing him. Schwarzenberg—the nominal commander-in-chief of the Allied armies—was a poor and extremely timid strategist under all circumstances, but in front of Napoleon he was apparently so awed that his habitual want of dash and hesitating slowness led him into an inordinate dissemination of his forces. In many ways he resembled some of the Austrian generals whom Napoleon had destroyed years before. He was, in fact just the sort of commander to give his great antagonist the opportunities he wanted and would be sure to make good use of. Blucher was a man of entirely different mettle: a soldier by instinct, a dashing leader by disposition and temper. Though old he was overflowing with energy. Not learned in the science of war he was apt to be rash, but his reckless daring was now kept within bounds by the highly educated Gneisenau and Muffling, who never left him.

The immediate object of the Allied sovereigns upon crossing the Rhine, was the occupation of Paris, but the general plan they adopted to secure it was extremely faulty. For the convenience of subsistence they unwisely distributed their armies over a wide front, as if there had been no great master of war within the zone of operations watching for an opportunity to beat them in detail. Instead of moving upon the enemy's capital by converging lines, so that Napoleon should not be able to seriously attack one without having the others on his flank, they marched with great intervals between their armies which were consequently unable to support one another. They entirely ignored the fact that the shortest and quickest and safest way to reach Paris was through the destruction of Napoleon's army. As they manœuvred they threw away to a large extent the only one great advantage they possessed—that of vastly superior numbers. Schwarzenberg's timid movements may or may not have been controlled by Metternich, but notwithstanding the many checks and defeats experienced by the Allies, as a matter of fact those defeats inflicted serious losses upon the French. Though often driven back the Allies always returned to their advance upon Paris with undiminished numbers and with the renewed energy which the arrival of reinforcements always imparts, whilst their opponent's army was dwindling away having no reserves to maintain it. But, as in the previous year, the Allies still feared to tackle any body of troops with which Napoleon was known to be present. They courted action with his Marshals, but the ascendency which his very name exercised over them was still enormous. Schwarzenberg's first idea was the safety of the Austrian army; and, feeling that he was no match for his great adversary, his mind seemed always more bent upon defensive than offensive combinations. He was not the man to conduct the invasion of France especially when Napoleon was in the field against him.

Let us now follow the general movements of the opposing forces.

Only two of the three armies of invasion, to which I have referred, marched for Paris—that of Schwarzenberg from Langres down the valley of the Seine to Troyes, and that of Blucher from Nancy to Joinville and down the Marne to St. Dizier. This separate line of advance was just what Napoleon most desired. It gave him the chance of beating first one then the other. Blucher's being the smaller body he turned first upon him. His plan was excellent; but it failed through one of those accidents which in war have so often frustrated the most ably devised schemes. An intercepted despatch disclosed the movement to the Allies. An indecisive action at Brienne, on January 28th, was succeeded by Napoleon's defeat at La Rothière on February 1st, where he lost heavily and had 54 guns and 3000 men taken by the enemy.

After this victory the Allies again separated their armies whilst Napoleon fell back upon Nogent. In the meantime, whilst Schwarzenberg was slowly and timidly following the retreating Emperor, Blucher was pushing past beyond him to the north making straight for Paris. In the haste of movement Blucher had, for the convenience of administration, broken up his army into detachments. Sacken with 15,000 men was at Ferté-sous-Jouarre; York's corps was disseminated along the road towards Chateau Thierry; 5000 Russians were at Champ-Aubert; and Blucher himself was at Fère-Champenoise with 20,000 men. Here was a great chance for a man of Napoleon's quick perception and decision. He first attacked and destroyed the Russians at Champ-Aubert, then turned upon Sacken whom he defeated with a loss of 26 guns and 4000 prisoners besides killed and wounded, the remnants of his force, together with York's corps, being driven by Mortier northwards towards Soissons. Marmont who, in full communication with Napoleon, had been slowly falling back before Blucher's own corps during these events was now joined by the Emperor. At Vauchamp Blucher found himself obliged to fall back and was vigorously pursued by Marmont who surprised and defeated his rearguard of Russians under Ourousoff. In this retreat Blucher lost 15 guns and 8000 men.

It was now Schwarzenberg's turn. With the main army he had advanced towards Paris as far as the River Yeres but was there held in check by Oudinot, Victor and Macdonald. Putting his guards into carts and carriages and marching night and day, Napoleon joined those Marshals on January 16th at Guignes. The following day he surprised the advance-guard of the Allies at Mormant, when this huge army fell back, pursued by Napoleon's handful of men, and did not halt till beyond Troyes.

This new condition of things weakened the Coalition, for each of the Allied sovereigns seemed more than ever to think of the position his own army would occupy at the end of the war rather than of the measures required to bring it to a conclusion. Each was intent upon what was to be his share in the plunder when the terms of peace were settled. The fact that certain provinces were actually held by the troops of any one particular Power when the cessation of hostilities came about would be a strong argument in favour of their retention by that Power. All were therefore anxious to place themselves in what would be the most advantageous position when the war should come to an end. Austria desired to secure large territory in Italy; but as, thanks to Eugène's skilful generalship, Italy had not yet been conquered Austrian statesmen had no desire whatever to bring about a premature peace. The real director of the Austrian army's movements at this time was not Schwarzenberg but the wily Metternich. That subtle and crafty statesman had negotiated the secession of Bavaria, Wurtemberg and Saxony, and he thought that Austria's claims to supersede France in the leadership of the states which had formed the Confederation of the Rhine should therefore be recognised. Having secured Murat's co-operation against his former master and benefactor he had every hope of being able in a short time to expel Eugène and occupy the Italian provinces. In order, however, to be in a position to enforce Austria's claims to these advantages it was necessary that the Austrian army should be kept as strong as possible. He was quite willing that Blucher, in his eagerness to seize Paris, should knock the Prussian and the Russian armies to pieces but he was determined that Schwarzenberg should do nothing of the kind with his army. The tardy appearance in Switzerland at this time of Augereau's corps in the rear of the Allies, came, therefore, as a convenient excuse for what was otherwise desirable—I mean, the further falling back of the Grand Army. The Allies of Austria were quite alive to the true nature of Metternich's policy and to the reasons which dictated it but they were not in a position to quarrel with her about it. They were consequently compelled to bend to the inevitable and devise a plan of campaign to accord with her obvious intentions.

Under strong pressure from England, Bernadotte had despatched from the north the corps of Woronzoff and Bulow to support Blucher in his next attempt to reach Paris by the valley of the Marne. The former joined Blucher when Wintzingerode's corps had taken possession of Soissons and St. Priest was bringing up a reinforcement of some 12,000 men through the

Ardennes and Chalons. Blucher's army, including these, was over 100,000 strong. It was now decided that Blucher should play the first and active part in the campaign whilst Schwarzenberg remained on the defensive: if Napoleon turned upon Blucher's army, the Grand Army under Schwarzenberg was to advance cautiously; disgusted as the other members of the Coalition were at such a plan of operations they were made to feel it was all they could expect from their Austrian allies.

Napoleon had arrived before Troyes on February 22nd; and on the 24th Blucher, without waiting to get his army in hand, pushed forward to attack Marmont on the Marne. Marmont fell back before the fiery Prussian towards La Ferté-sous-Jouarre. There he was within supporting distance by Mortier, who had been watching Wintzingerode, who had moved from Soissons to Rheims, and Bulow who had reached Laon. As soon as Wintzingerode had quitted Soissons Mortier recaptured it and placed in it a fairly strong garrison under General Moreau.* Mortier and Marmont together could only muster 12,000 men but by a skilful use of the Marne and the Ourcq they checked Blucher's advance beyond the latter river till March 1st, when they were reinforced by 6,000 men from Paris.

Meanwhile Napoleon, leaving Troyes on February 27th, hastened with 25,000 men to the support of his Marshals and was at Ferté-sous-Jouarre, in Blucher's

---

* This General Moreau must not be confounded with Napoleon's old rival for power, who had been killed the previous year by a chance round shot.

rear, by March 1st. Napoleon's prospects of dealing Blucher a deadly blow now seemed most brilliant, and he must have felt as if he had him already in the hollow of his hand. Blucher had no choice but to retreat in all haste northwards by way of Soissons. But Napoleon knew that it was held by Moreau and that its defences had recently been improved. He at once pushed Marmont and Mortier in pursuit and on March 3rd crossed the Marne with his own force in support of them. Blucher had called to him Wintzingerode and also Bulow who had arrived *via* Holland and Belgium and who, upon reaching Soissons, had induced Moreau to surrender just at the moment when Napoleon was expecting to gain the full advantage of a fortified post on Blucher's only possible line of retreat. It is difficult to say what might have happened had Moreau done his duty; for, with an army recently defeated to be forced across an unfordable river by an antagonist of Napoleon's calibre is an ugly business under all circumstances. It is certain that Moreau was not a traitor but he was a weak-kneed creature unworthy of any responsibility in war. Napoleon was furious, and most justly so, when he heard the news. "Have that miserable creature arrested," he wrote, "and also the members of the council of defence: have them arraigned before a Military Commission consisting of general officers, and, in God's name, see that they are shot in twenty-four hours." Had Moreau held out for a day and a half longer than he did I cannot see how Blucher could have escaped an overwhelming disaster. Thiers refers to this surrender in his usual inflated terms as, next to

Waterloo, the most fatal event in French history. This may be a great exaggeration ; but, as far as the war of 1814 in France was concerned, it is not too much to say that Napoleon's star set when Soissons surrendered. No such other opportunity again presented itself in this campaign.

## CHAPTER IV.

### THE CAMPAIGN OF 1814—*continued*.

ON the night of March 3rd Blucher safely crossed the Aisne and took up a position between Craonne and Soissons along its northern bank. Napoleon, crossing that same river at Berry-au-Bac in advance of his Marshals, who were engaged in an unsuccessful attempt on Soissons, turned Blucher's left, defeated Woronsoff at Craonne and pushed on by the Soissons road to Laon, whither Blucher, on finding his left turned, had withdrawn his whole army.

The battle of Laon followed on March 9th. Marmont's attack from the south-east had been fairly successful during the day, as Blucher, under the impression that there must be some central body between Marmont and Napoleon who was advancing from the south-west, hesitated to attack. Having at last discovered his mistake he fell upon Marmont's bivouacs by night and nearly destroyed him, taking 45 guns and 2,500 prisoners. It was a tremendous blow to Napoleon at this stage of his fortunes; but, far from succumbing to it he resolved to continue his own attack upon Laon the following day. He had less than 20,000 men, but he calculated that, in order to make sure of success in his attack upon Marmont, Blucher must have seriously reduced the force now opposed to himself. It was not until he had ascertained that Blucher was concentrating all his force with the intention of falling upon him that he at last yielded

TALLEYRAND.

to the entreaties of his Marshals and fell back upon Soissons. Before as well as after the battle of Laon it was of importance to Napoleon that he should husband his resources in every possible way. As a matter of abstract prudence, therefore, it could not have been wise of him to attack an enemy nearly threefold his strength and in a good defensive position. Besides, he would have been the first to have condemned any of his Marshals who had allowed, as he had done, one fraction of his army to advance by the road from Soissons to Laon while the other marched by a road beyond all supporting distance from it—that is, by the road from Berry-au-Bac to that same town. The point of concentration was also known to be in occupation of the enemy—a fact which rendered the operation still more dangerous and still further opposed to the well-understood maxims of war. This northern movement upon Soissons and Laon cost Napoleon and the Allies about 12,000 men each; but whilst the former could not replace his loss the latter were at once able to do so. Blucher lost a great chance at Laon for had he but launched the whole of his troops upon Napoleon, it is difficult to see how the little French army in his front could have been saved from utter destruction. But it has been well said indeed of all the contests in this campaign that the great Corsican's presence, like Medusa's head, invariably paralysed as well as terrorised his enemies.

In the several rapid movements he made from one flank to the other of the theatre of war, Napoleon had seldom with him more than about 25,000 men. Each time that he marched from right to left or *vice versâ*, he was of course compelled to leave behind a sufficient number to conceal his departure from whatever Allied forces had been in front of him, and also to make head against them should they assume an active offensive in his absence. Rumour, however, always greatly exaggerated his numbers and he took every care to do so himself by all possible methods. Indeed, his movements were so extremely rapid that he never gave the enemy time to ascertain his real strength for his practice always was to strike at once when he reached the hostile forces. An exaggerated notion of his numbers was therefore easily fostered. His audacity in striking with his little army at part of Schwarzenberg's vast host of 120,000 men was of itself sufficient to make his opponents believe that he was strong, for it was not thought he would venture upon such daring operations unless he had a powerful army behind him. Throughout this phase of the campaign he relied almost entirely upon his own skill in handling troops; he looked to the terror of his name to keep him out of serious danger whilst he trusted greatly to his luck and to Schwarzenberg's bungling and cautious slowness for opportunities to pull the chestnuts from between the bars before the fire could touch them.

On March 11th the Russian general St. Priest took the fortified town of Rheims by sudden assault during the night—a place of considerable strategic importance at the moment as its possession re-established communications between the still widely separated armies of Blucher and Schwarzenberg. St. Priest, foolishly believing that Napoleon's army had been destroyed by Blucher at Laon, billeted his 15,000 men in the villages round Rheims and took little or no precautions to protect them from surprise. Napoleon, aware of St. Priest's isolated position, moved secretly and by forced marches upon Rheims, and on March 13th retook the town and drove him in great disorder and with great loss from the neighbourhood.

This reappearance of Napoleon on the field of battle at a moment when the Allies had begun to think his end had come drew from one of his distinguished opponents the following remarks: "We expect to see this terrible man everywhere. He has beaten us all, one after the other: we dread the audacity of his enterprises the rapidity of his movements and his able combinations. One has scarcely conceived any scheme of operations before he destroys it."

Napoleon's fierce attack upon Laon, his practical destruction of St. Priest and his bold stay at Rheims close to Blucher's position on the Aisne were not without their effect. We find that, notwithstanding the great Prussian general's feverish anxiety to finish the war, he did not again venture to move southwards beyond that river until March 20th—until, in fact, he knew that Napoleon had quitted Rheims. Napoleon halted at that place from March 14th to 17th; and on the latter date, gathering in some fresh reinforcements, marched to Epernay in order to threaten Schwarzenberg who had only ventured to advance beyond Troyes when he heard, on the 14th, of Napoleon's repulse at Laon. But the Austrian commander-in-chief moved slowly and cautiously driving before him Macdonald and Oudinot who had been left to watch him. As soon, however, as he heard that Napoleon had reached Epernay he again took alarm and again fell back pursued in hot haste by Napoleon, who made for Arcès-sur-Aube full of confidence notwithstanding his very great inferiority in strength.

A sudden change now came over the plans of the Allies. The Czar had long inwardly chafed at the repeated retreats and uncertain movements of the Allied forces whenever and wherever Napoleon made his appearance, even with the most insignificant numbers. The fear that Austria might withdraw from the Coalition had now passed away; for by a new treaty each nation had pledged itself not to make any treaty without the consent of the other Allied powers. The Emperor Alexander consequently felt that he might now safely insist upon a sounder and more active military policy. The result was an order issued to all the component parts of the Allied army under Schwarzenberg's command to march northwards, and, having joined hands with Blucher, to press on direct for Paris as one concentrated army no matter what Napoleon might do. The Allied army was engaged in striving to effect this intended concentration near Arcès when Napoleon took up his position there. He soon found himself nearly hemmed in and with difficulty effected his retreat across the Aube. In order to secure the bridges he had himself to dismount and, sword in hand, rally the fugitives.

His fortunes now appeared to be almost at their last ebb. He had the advantage of operating upon interior lines and of interposing between the two great masses into which the invading army was divided, but yet he had been roughly and with great loss repulsed by both. He clearly saw that they were at last bent upon closing in upon him to crush him between them. In the south Wellington had beaten Soult at Orthez and was advancing on Toulouse, having despatched Beresford to Bordeaux where he had been received with enthusiasm; and La Vendée was moving in behalf of the Bourbons. He was begirt with enemies and his friends were only half-hearted, yet he did not despair. The calmness with which he faced disaster, the resource and ingenuity with which he contrived to find hope and almost substantial grounds for hope, is most remarkable. Think what we may of him personally, we cannot refuse to admire the magnificent courage and indomitable spirit of this self-contained giant of strength and superhuman genius.

He could no longer oppose the direct advance of the Allies upon Paris; but there was still one course open to him: he might fall upon their lines of communication with all the troops he could collect whilst Joseph did his best to defend the capital. He calculated that there had been already time for the recovery and convalescence of the invalids thrown into the great frontier fortresses of Luxembourg, Verdun, Metz, Thionville, etc., etc., and also for the tolerable training of many conscripts within those places. These fresh troops would swell his ranks and the possession of those fortresses for purposes of supply would enable him to move with great freedom. By this daring operation he hoped to relieve Paris of all or at least of any serious pressure upon it. This calculation was based upon the supposition that, in accordance with all tradition all theory and all precedent in formally conducted armies, the Allies would conceive it to be an unquestioned necessity to fall back in order to restore and protect their communications with the Rhine which Napoleon had fallen upon and cut off. He also attached great importance to the moral effect which this startling and very bold combination would have upon his own soldiers as well as upon the enemy. But its success depended upon the defence of Paris by Joseph until Napoleon had had time to reach the valley of the Meuse with all his available forces. This was the weak point in his scheme ; for his poor feeble brother was a broken reed to rest upon, and he had not even taken any effective steps to place Paris beyond the danger of a *coup de main*.

When Napoleon started from Arcès-sur-Aube in the direction of Vitri and St. Dizier, to carry out his new and daring project, his numbers were too small to enable him to act successfully upon the enemy's rear. He had consequently to draw to himself Pacthod's division, then at Bergères, and the corps of Marmont and Mortier which he had left to watch Blucher when he turned south to fall upon Schwarzenberg. But in taking these troops with him he withdrew from the neighbourhood of Paris the only really good corps allotted for its defence and upon which its safety most depended. As Blucher had advanced they had fallen back in a south-westerly direction towards the capital and had reached Fère-en-Tardenois when they received Napoleon's order to join him at St. Dizier by way of Chalons. Had these orders reached them before Blucher, in his southward movement to join Schwarzenberg, had reached a position to the eastward of them they could easily have complied ; but, as it was, their only chance of doing so then was by a cross-country road to Vitri.

For the second time in this campaign an intercepted despatch disclosed the Emperor's project to the enemy. Anxious to keep up the failing spirits of the dejected court in Paris, he had written his wife a full account of the project which he still hoped would restore his fortunes. And this it was that fell into the enemy's hands on March 24th.

As long as Blucher and Schwarzenberg had operated independently against Paris with a great interval between their armies, the central line, that between Paris and Chalons, was generally available for Napoleon's movements. This was, he deemed, all the safer now since he had driven those two hostile armies so wide apart. Not only had he consequently ordered Marmont and Mortier to use it in coming to him but other troops were then marching westward by it. General Compans with about three thousand men had reached La Ferté *en route* to join him by Sezanne. Two divisions of the National Guard were nearing Chalons with a large convoy of artillery. All these detachments, in ignorance of their danger, were moving independently between the two Allied armies, whose presence they were not aware of, whilst Napoleon at the same moment was farther from Paris than either Blucher or Schwarzenberg. This was a very dangerous condition of things for the French.

When the full nature of Napoleon's scheme became known to the Allies, Blucher at once resolved that instead of pressing south-westwards by himself

RETREAT OF NAPOLEON ON PARIS—CAMPAIGN OF 1814.

[*To face page* 112.

towards Paris he would march direct upon Chalons to ensure his junction with Schwarzenberg in the great open country between it and Vitri. Having begun this movement, he despatched at the same time a large force of cavalry and horse artillery under Wintzingerode towards St. Dizier. This he did in order to conceal the intended movement of the two concentrated armies upon Paris which was now laid open to them by Napoleon's movement towards Chaumont and the Upper Meuse. Schwarzenberg at first was somewhat alarmed by the news contained in the intercepted despatch; but as one consequence of Napoleon's movement on St. Dizier and thence southwards upon Doulevent, the French cavalry had chased from Chaumont and Bar-sur-Aube the Allied diplomatic headquarters with the Emperor of Austria and Metternich. They had fled to Dijon. Schwarzenberg was by this relieved of the clog upon all his plans and movements which their vicinity had proved; and as he could no longer, for the time at least, appeal to the authority of his court he consented to the now strongly expressed desire of the Czar that the Grand Army should at once join Blucher and that the two armies so united should march direct upon Paris, regardless of what Napoleon might do. The Allied forces having effected their junction as intended moved forward at last for Paris on March 24th, as one vast force, to the delight of all the soldiers in those armies. Its advance was in two columns covered by great masses of horsemen, who on the 25th upon reaching Soudé-Sainte-Croix—about half-way between Vitri and Fère Champenoise—

struck upon Marmont's camp just as Mortier's columns had reached it. Those two Marshals were very roughly handled and driven back in the utmost disorder upon Fère Champenoise, and finally upon Allemant near Sezanne. The French troops as a body had not behaved well this day and their losses were very heavy. Whilst the Marshals were so engaged, a great artillery-train together with a large ammunition and provision convoy, also bound for Napoleon's camp, came upon the scene to the northward. Abandoned to its fate by the flying troops under Marmont and Mortier, and overwhelmed on all sides by cavalry and horse artillery, it was totally destroyed. Altogether, the French loss this day amounted to 60 guns and about 10,000 men.

Cut off from all possibility of joining Napoleon and almost surrounded by enemies, the defeated Marshals had to make a wide détour by Melun in order to get back between Paris and the now steadily advancing and concentrated Allied armies. They reached Charenton—to the south-east of the city—at midday on March 29th.

By that date the Allies also had reached the neighbourhood of the capital upon its northern and eastern sides. The Empress and the Council of Regency escaped to Blois in accordance with Napoleon's instructions, leaving Joseph to provide for the defence of the city. Nothing could have been more feeble than his conduct in this emergency. The force at his disposal consisted of some cadres of the Guard into which at the last moment he had poured some thousands of conscripts. Marmont and Mortier had brought back about 12,000 men and Compans, lately reinforced by a few battalions, was in command of some 6000 more. General Money had taken command of about 5000 of the National Guard who had been lately organised. There was a large quantity of heavy guns available, but no adequate steps had been taken to place them in position or to establish any defensive works on the commanding heights round Paris. We often hear much ignorant ridicule of permanent fortifications and this is a good illustration of how foolish it sometimes is ; for if in 1814 that city had been protected by external forts, as in 1870, the result of this campaign might have been very different. But far-seeing as Napoleon generally was he had not contemplated the possibility—until too late—of Paris, the centre and focus of his power, being assailed by an enemy. Had he even in the month of January constructed great field works on the east and north and south of Paris and thickly armed them with heavy guns, the city might have held out whilst he, in the valley of the Meuse, made havoc of his enemies' lines of communication.

The Allies pressed forward upon the north of Paris on a front extending from the St. Denis (Bois de Boulogne) road eastward to Belleville and Romainville, and upon March 30th drove the French from all their forward positions into the city. Joseph then authorised Marmont to negotiate for the evacuation of the place, and by the evening of that same day a convention having been agreed to, all hostilities ceased.

Meanwhile Napoleon's cavalry had actually seized Chaumont directly on Schwarzenberg's line of communication. He was himself at Doulevent on March 25th, anxiously awaiting the arrival of Marmont and Mortier on the very day of their great disaster when it was reported to him that large masses of the enemy's cavalry were in sight. For the moment no news could have pleased him better, for it seemed to imply that, as he had calculated upon, Schwarzenberg was falling back to restore his communications. He at once moved to the attack with all the forces he had at hand, hoping to cut his way through the hostile horse and join hands with the Marshals whom he hourly expected. This cavalry of the enemy was under Wintzingerode, and over it he gained a brilliant success driving it at last with great loss to the northeast far off the immediate zone of operations and beyond Bar le Duc. It was from his prisoners he then first gathered some indication of what had happened. In the first place he was startled to find that it was with Blucher's and not with Schwarzenberg's army he had been fighting. Secondly, they all reported vague rumours of the Allies' march upon Paris. It became therefore vitally important he should ascertain the facts.

Halting himself at St. Dizier, he pushed a strong reconnaissance forward to Vitri on the 26th. From it for the first time he heard of the Marshal's defeat at Fère-Champenoise on the 25th, and also that Talleyrand and his party had summoned the Allies to Paris, whither they had marched.

Even after the reception of this news his own inclination was to adhere to his plan for moving on the enemy's communications with every man he could collect, leaving the Allies to do their worst upon Paris. But the series of disasters his arms had sustained during the last three campaigns had robbed him of much of his old undisputed sway. Most of his generals were despondent—Berthier, his chief of the staff, most so. All agreed that he must either save Paris or succumb. The pressure brought to bear by those about him was now too strong to be resisted. Two years before he would have summarily dismissed the man who ventured unasked to give him any advice at all. Besides, he began to realise that Paris could not hold out long enough against the Allies' overwhelming numbers to enable him to attack and spread disorder in the enemy's rear. He consequently hurried back towards Paris with all the troops he could take with him in one of his rapid, relayed marches. Travelling post, and moving by Troyes, he reached Fontainebleau on March 31st. There he learnt that Paris had surrendered, but even yet he was by no means disposed to give up the game. On the very day of his arrival he addressed a despatch to the Empress telling her of the rising *en masse* of the eastern provinces, of the capture of all sorts of distinguished people when his cavalry broke in upon the diplomatic headquarters, etc., etc. He went upon the plan of telling untruths without hesitation when he thought it advisable to spread abroad the most flattering stories of his victories and of the losses inflicted upon the enemy.

Paris being now lost to him, he makes arrangements for prosecuting the war with Orleans as his new base and new seat of government. Orders were issued for the concentration of all his forces, both those which fell back from Paris upon its surrender and those which had been following his rapid movements; they were to take up a position south of Paris between it and Essonne. He provides for the reorganisation of the civil government, appointing special prefects and other administrative officers to assist him in carrying on the war upon which he is still bent.

But able as his conceptions are, clever and business-like as are all his arrangements, he is no longer the absolute monarch who can feel certain of his orders being obeyed. His Guards and the privates and under-officers generally are still faithful and will follow him anywhere; but the Marshals whom he has raised from the ranks, and the Senate whose members owe their places and fortunes to him, all have determined, and wisely determined for the sake of France, that the war shall end—that there shall be peace no matter how destructive its terms may be to the master who had made them. Amongst the many ways in which the personal loyalty of the rank and file to Napoleon at this juncture shows in strong contrast with the calculated treason of his generals, the following story is a good illustration: Marmont, acting within his right—within his duty in fact—entered into negotiations for himself and on behalf of his corps that they would abide by the decree of the Senate. When on April 2nd that body declared the Emperor deposed and nominated a Provisional Government, Marmont issued orders on the assumption that his men felt as he did. But when they and their regimental officers learned that the intention was to abandon Napoleon they refused to obey. Marmont was riding towards his corps when the generals met him and told him this news, warning him at the same time that he would certainly be shot if he appeared on parade. He was too brave a man to fear his own soldiers so he rode in amongst them. After a very French scene where everybody seems to have cried together he succeeded in carrying his corps with him and led them into the camp of the Allies.

For some time there was much talk of a Regency under the Empress until Napoleon's son was old enough to reign, but all felt that this would only mean Napoleon under a new guise. Even he himself scoffed at the notion of a Regency under a child, as he called his wife. The only other alternative was the restoration of the Bourbons, and for this the Allies declared. As Talleyrand well said, "the Regency was an intrigue, the Bourbons alone were a principle."

It was his Marshals who forced Napoleon to abdicate. They were sick of war, had drunk deep of its glory and had exhausted all the rewards it was in the power of their great leader to bestow. For the ten previous years many of them had not spent as many months at home. The story of Marmont's desertion of the master who had raised him to a great position would require an article to itself. Whatever posterity may think of its morality, there can be no doubt that it was the final blow which destroyed Napoleon in 1814. We are asked by some historians to condemn these men because the sovereign they destroyed had covered them with wealth and honours ;

but it must not be forgotten that they had then to decide between fidelity to him and loyalty to their country. Who can therefore justly blame them? Not surely those whose ancestors deserted James II. and joined the great William of Nassau because the welfare of England depended upon the success of the Revolution!

On April 5th and 6th Napoleon urged his Marshals to follow him behind the Loire and continue the struggle. He appealed to their loyalty and to those feelings which attach soldiers to great leaders; but all in vain. As scheme upon scheme was projected in that colossal, that labyrinthine mind of his, how the iron must have entered into his soul as he, the "man of thousand thrones," was forced to listen to his Marshals, his former humble servants, when they declared in tones of dictation and of menace that he must abdicate unconditionally for they would take no part in the civil war which his proposed action would entail upon France! Convinced as many are that the campaign of 1814 was not only a folly but a crime, still one cannot contemplate Napoleon's last week at Fontainebleau without the deepest feeling of pity for his lot. And who can withhold his admiration of the sterling courage, the honest fidelity and simple loyalty of the rank and file to the master who had so often led them to victory? Although we may feel that he was little worthy of their noble devotion, who will deny his meed of praise to the humble, warm-hearted and gallant French soldier for bestowing it upon the idol of his life?

As soon as it became generally known at Fontainebleau that Napoleon had abdicated he was deserted by his generals and by nearly all his staff, and very few officers remained even to do duty at his headquarters.

On April 11th Napoleon issued an address to the army that had remained faithful to him, spoke his famous farewell to his Generals and signed his Act of Abdication. The Allies gave him the pleasant little island of Elba as his future residence and allowed him to play there at royalty under the title of Emperor, with a small party of his Guards and such of his courtiers as wished to accompany him into exile. These easy terms entailed upon the world a risk of war which the Allies were not justified in permitting. He was the Peace-Destroyer of Europe and his reappearance in France at any time would mean more war, more misery to nations, his own adopted nation included. Having at last, after great suffering and exertions, caught this unrivalled bird of prey they should not have contented themselves with any mere clipping of his wings: they should have pinioned him and have closely caged him, as they subsequently did at St. Helena, and taken every precaution, no matter how inconvenient to him, to render his escape impossible. Had he been in their place no sentimental feeling for fallen greatness, for defeated royalty would have influenced his decision; his knowledge of human nature, his practical common sense would have told him that Napoleon Bonaparte was not the man to remain long a prisoner in a little island from which escape was comparatively easy. Had proper precautions been taken in 1814 to prevent his ever again troubling the world, what an amount of bloodshed and of consequent misery the Allies would have saved Europe, what defeat and further abasement they would have spared France!

Wellington's final stroke which shattered Soult's army at Toulouse was not delivered until six days after the date of Napoleon's abdication, so slowly in those days did news travel. Soult had heard vague rumours of what had taken place at Paris and Fontainebleau but had received no official authority for a suspension of arms.

And so ended the much-talked-of and very remarkable campaign of 1814. Until the Napoleonic idea, so fostered by the writings of M. Thiers, had led France into the war of 1870 it was the common study of all military students as a brilliant example of the offensive-defensive. It is full of instruction for soldiers, and also abounds in incidents that are fitting subjects for the high-flown exaggeration of the grandiloquent French historian in his description of the wounded tiger's death-struggle; woe betide the man who dared to approach within reach of even his crippled strength! But looking at it from the standpoint of French patriotism—if an Englishman can do so—one feels obliged to condemn it as a campaign that should never have taken place. The odds against Napoleon when he determined upon it, were so overwhelming that nothing short of a miracle in his favour could have secured him eventual success. We admire, we praise the man who when fighting solely for his country fights to the last trusting to some chance miracle to give her

PORTO FERRAJO, ELBA.

the victory. But no one can be justified in fighting out a war to the bitter end, as Napoleon did in 1814, when that war is waged for his own reasons and his own personal objects.

In the actual theatre of war Napoleon's strategy for the first three months of this year is beyond all praise. But as a campaign, as a great episode in this three years' war, it was based upon a thoroughly unsound military policy. When he made up his mind to refuse the terms offered by the Allies before they had crossed the Rhine he should have secured to himself all the possible chances in his favour. I have already referred to the garrisons in Germany and to his armies in Spain which he might have withdrawn. Why not at once have sent back to Madrid his prisoner, the real king of Spain, having made an advantageous peace with him? This and his deposition of Joseph, the poor unmilitary creature to whom he had given that historic crown, would have gone far towards conciliating what I may term the spirit the sentiment of Divine Right to which the Allied sovereigns attached considerable weight. It would certainly have tended to make some of them half-hearted in the contest and to weaken still more the ties which kept the Alliance together. Had he wished he might—immediately after Dresden—have easily detached his father-in-law, the Emperor of Austria, from the Coalition. Indeed, whilst freely admitting that the whole strategic conception of the campaigns of 1813 and 1814 was of the highest order, the general military policy, largely based upon the unexpected chances of the game, which he then pursued was faulty in the extreme; and if an ordinary individual may venture to question the wisdom of the man whom he believes to have been the greatest of God's human creations, it was opposed to the interests of exhausted France and most hurtful to what was still dearer to him—I mean his own interests. Many of the battles in this campaign are splendid examples of Napoleon's best style of fighting and of his master-genius in war, but they must not be confounded with victories. They are so styled by M. Thiers and his school; but beyond the glory which some of them shed upon him and the French army at the time, each battle was little more than a serious reduction of his already attenuated forces—that is, of his power to continue the struggle against the practically inexhaustible strength of the Allied armies then converging upon Paris. The game played by the invaders was a game of attrition reminding us very much of that played by General Grant when brought face to face with Lee, the Napoleon in ability of the American civil war. Like General Grant, the Allies were always ready to lose one thousand of their men if they could only kill half that number of their enemies.

In 1814 Napoleon's army was a mixture of seasoned soldiers and young conscripts in a proportion of about one to five, and France has good reason to be proud of them for all alike fought well. When overpowered and beaten they did not condescend to attribute their defeat—as under the Second Empire—to the treason of their leaders. But let us at once disabuse ourselves of the notion that they were fighting for France.

They fought for and at the bidding of the man Napoleon Bonaparte, the great the magnificent Emperor who had inundated France with glory—with a glory that has never been surpassed and which possibly may never again be equalled.

The Allies set to work in the Congress of Vienna to provide for the disposition of what had once been Napoleon's empire and there was much bickering over the spoils. The Bourbons and the returned *emigrés* settled down to govern France again as if no Napoleon had ever been born, certainly as if he no longer existed. But the heterogeneous elements in France, the survival of the Revolution as well as of the Empire, were quite beyond the power of their narrow minds to grasp, much less to deal with effectively. The strong hand of a soldier-dictator like Napoleon was required to control them. The task was far beyond the powers of the few returned nobles and the handful of lawyers who now essayed to govern France under a new Bourbon king. But it would be beyond the scope of my subject to deal with that interesting and complicated story. Suffice it to say that it was the quarrels of the Powers assembled in Congress at Vienna and the manifest incapacity of the Bourbons and of their followers to satisfy and control France, that eventually gave another opportunity to the great Soldier-King whose first fall I have here endeavoured to describe. Of his wonderful resurrection for the one hundred days which ended at Waterloo I shall speak in the following chapters.

## CHAPTER V.

### THE HUNDRED DAYS.—THE BATTLE OF LIGNY.

AT one o'clock in the afternoon of March 1st, 1815, three little ships cast anchor in the Gulf of St. Juan. They carried the great Napoleon who, with some eleven hundred of his finest soldiers, had escaped from Elba, his badly-guarded prison-house, only a few days before. For purposes of battle this handful of men would have been useless but they were invaluable to protect their master from police interference during his advance upon Paris.

His return to France was not influenced by any deep patriotic motive but was the outcome of a fiendish and inordinate ambition of the most selfish kind. It meant a new outburst of war, more bloodshed and a fresh crop of misery to Europe. France required peace above all things after her many years of Revolutionary horrors and devastating strife; but Napoleon from Elba brought her war with England and every Continental State. His return begat new trials and new sufferings for humanity.

The troops sent by Lewis XVIII. to oppose his advance upon Paris greeted him with shouts of *Vive l'Empereur*. Even the chivalrous Ney, who had sworn allegiance to his new master, the Bourbon King, was drawn into the great military whirlpool of revolt and declared for the leader whose fortunes he had so long followed both in sunshine and in gloom.

Napoleon entered Paris on March 21st, his journey having been a sort of royal and triumphal progress. When he reached the Tuileries he had good reason for saying to Caulincourt that the success of his rash venture was a return once more of that dazzling good-fortune which had spoiled him during so many years.

As soon as it was known at Vienna that Napoleon had landed in France the Plenipotentiaries, there assembled in Congress, issued a formal notice of outlawry against him. In it they declared that "as an enemy and disturber of the tranquillity of the world he is abandoned to public vengeance." All European countries rang with the call to arms to crush this tyrant this peace destroyer whom no Treaties could bind. To help the nations of Europe, England promised to pay them monthly, in proportion to their armies, a total amount of over £11,000,000 sterling.

Napoleon's first great want was time: to re-establish his authority reorganise his government and create a new army that would enable him to meet his enemies in the field. He strove to divide the Coalition against him by an endeavour to treat separately with each of the Allied Powers. But they were not to be taken in by his specious declarations and refused even to receive his Envoys.

He had hoped that, once in the Tuileries again as the accepted Sovereign of the people he would be able to take up the reins of government and rule as before. He felt that it was only as Dictator he could hope to steer France safely through the thousand dangers with which his return surrounded her. A wise man of action he was neither the fool nor the criminal to imagine that the talkers and thinkers of the Senate or those who in the Lower House babbled of liberty and argued about the abstract principles of parliamentary government were the men to rule France at such a conjuncture. Had those who then directed her destinies been wise and sincerely and heartily in his favour they would with one voice have hailed him as Dictator. But he soon found that nothing was then further from their thoughts. To his soldiers he was still the Emperor as of yore but the jabbering dreamers in both Houses of Parliament persisted in regarding him as merely the elected head of a constitutional monarchy. The very men he had chosen to be his ministers would not have him as Dictator, and his brother Lucien—the irreconcilable Republican—was openly opposed to any re-establishment of the Empire upon its former basis. He soon realised that until victory had decked him with a new aureole of Imperial authority he could not hope to be again the undisputed ruler of France unless indeed he would stoop to appeal to the worst passions of the people generally. He knew that with the military sentiment of the country in his favour he might easily arouse such a crusade against the rich the privileged classes and all those who cried for a Bourbon King, that he might at once become again the unquestioned and all-powerful despot. But his experience of the Revolution horrors in his young days had given him a rooted loathing of unbridled democracy and of mob rule. As he said at St. Helena he had no wish or intention to be the King of a modern Jacquerie.

As he would not be such a King and could not be again the absolute Emperor the only line open to him was that of Constitutional Sovereign—a position which his advisers urged him to assume. His first and most urgent want was an army sufficiently large to destroy his enemies in the field and to obtain this he felt he must bend before the pressure of his friends. Promises always sat lightly upon him and he was now prepared to promise anything if they would only give him what he needed at the moment. In order therefore to satisfy popular opinion he promulgated, on April 22nd, a form of Constitution which on nearly all important points closely resembled the Charter that had been recently published by Lewis XVIII. But it is not too much to say that this Constitution would not have been worth the paper it was written on had he returned triumphant to Paris after Waterloo. He would then have quickly and rudely silenced those who dared to babble of liberal and parliamentary institutions. For the moment, however, it answered his purpose. Indeed many were even foolish enough to believe the statement in his new charter to the effect that he had formerly postponed the introduction of free institutions into France in order to establish a great federal system in Europe; that he was anxious to establish such a system because he had always thought it would lead generally to progress and civilisation, but that at any rate he would in future restrict his efforts to increase prosperity and strengthen public liberty at home. How he must have laughed inwardly as he wrote this!

Both Houses of his Parliament went out of their way to remind him that he was merely the head of a constitutionally governed country: that the two Chambers were national and representative institutions and no longer Napoleonic clubs as formerly. To us now their addresses read as childishly comic; by him they were simply regarded as impertinent. In one of his dignified answers he told them: "It is in times of difficulty that great nations, like great men unfold all the energy of their character and become objects of admiration to posterity!" He warned them not to imitate the example of the leaders of the Byzantine empire who had made themselves for ever the laughing-stock of posterity by persisting in the discussion of subtle abstract points of constitutional procedure at a time when the barbarians were pressing them on all sides and at the very moment even when their battering-rams were breaking down the gates of the capital. But much as he hated liberty in every form, he did not then feel strong enough to dismiss his half-hearted advisers upon the eve of that war with all Europe which his escape from Elba had entailed upon France. What were his inward reservations when he swore to abide by this new constitution may be judged from what he said aloud: "I am not the man to permit a pack of lawyers to make my laws for me nor to allow the factions to cut off my head."

Napoleon's reconquest of France was thus achieved without bloodshed; but it was more the unpopularity of the Bourbons than his own claims upon the people's love which secured him this easy success. Their conduct had been as foolish as it was unstatesmanlike. Napoleon said justly of them that they had learnt nothing from past experience and had forgotten nothing. In heaping rewards and favours upon their loyal adherents from whom they had nothing to fear, they neglected, offended, and even oppressed their enemies the children of the Revolution, who could alone have kept them on the throne. They ignored the effect which had been worked in the mind and sentiment of the people by the Revolution as well as by the glory, renown and pride with which its heir— Napoleon—had covered every individual Frenchman. Their adherents, the returned *emigrés*, seemed to treat all who were not Royalists as enemies and to regard France as a country they had reconquered. So strong was the anti-Bourbon feeling, especially in Paris, that even if Napoleon had not escaped from Elba it is tolerably certain a new revolution would soon have chased Lewis XVIII. from the throne and made Lewis-Philip king. Napoleon said of himself, that upon reaching Paris it was not Lewis but the Duke of Orleans he had dethroned. The thousands of regimental officers of all grades who had been dismissed by the new king from the army to starve on pittances that would not have supported so many mechanics, were about the most dangerous men to the Bourbon cause. All of them hailed Napoleon's return with transports of joy. There were also thousands in every class who, during the Revolution, having purchased property belonging to the nobles and to the Church lived in dread of having it taken from them by the Royalists. Napoleon quieted their fears by confirming them in its possession—a popular act which secured him a considerable following among the men of influence and property.

From the hour of his arrival in Paris he worked like a galley-slave. Few men indeed in the world's history have effected in the same space of time anything to be compared with what he accomplished during the eighty-four days of his stay there. He had to re-establish his authority all over France, to tranquillise the country generally, put down Royalist risings, obtain money for his military wants, adjust the national finances and restore the civil administration everywhere. All this he had to do at a time when the whole of his energies were required to raise, organise and supply with all fighting requisites an army sufficiently large to enable him to meet Europe in arms with any chance of success.

He succeeded in finding over £3,000,000 by Extraordinary Loans and by forestalling the revenue of future years. With this sum and about half that amount which he found in the Treasury he was able to fully equip the army of 200,000 men with which he was about to take the field against Blucher and Wellington in Flanders.

Whilst he was thus busily employed preparing for the coming struggle the Allies on their side had been slowly gathering their forces against him. Vast armies of Russians, Austrians and Germans were in movement towards the Rhine, and there were already assembled in Belgium a heterogeneous army of

Belgians, Dutch, Hanoverians, Germans and Englishmen under Wellington, and if not a very good at least a homogeneous Prussian army under Blucher. For facility of feeding and supply, the troops of these two armies in Belgium were, however, so scattered in cantonments over a wide extent of country that it would take at least four days to concentrate them for battle between Brussels and the French frontier. But the fact is, the Allies did not expect Napoleon to assume the offensive in June and all their plans were made with a view to their own invasion of France later on, but certainly not before July 1st, with an immense army made up of Russians and Austrians as well as of those nations already represented by the Allied armies in Belgium.

Strange to say the full story of this Waterloo campaign, the shortest and yet one of the most decisive in our history, has yet to be written. It may be said to have only lasted five—one might almost say only four—days. Napoleon left Paris on June 12th for the valley of the Sambre and was back there again on the 21st as a fallen and defeated monarch.

Nelson's glorious victory at Trafalgar saved England from invasion by a great and splendid army under the first of all commanders, and it must consequently be for ever regarded by us as an event of the first importance in our history. But Wellington's victory at Waterloo concerned the whole civilised world and was fraught with the paramount import of life and death to many European powers. The interests involved in that one battle exceeded all that in modern history, before or since, have ever depended upon one day's fighting. Yet it is not difficult to explain the causes which, until quite recent years, have prevented the whole truth about it being generally known. During this campaign there was

NELSON.

considerable friction between Wellington and Blucher's Chief of the Staff, Count Gneisenau, who had long been prejudiced against our great Duke. Circumstances connected with the battle of Waterloo and the events immediately preceding it—to which I shall allude presently—tended to strengthen this angry feeling. On the other hand nothing could exceed Prince Blucher's loyalty to Wellington; and Baron Müffling, the Prussian representative at the English headquarters, united with the Prince in his profound admiration for the Duke. Müffling, who disliked Gneisenau and was fully aware of his feelings on this point, was most anxious after Waterloo, in the interests of both countries, to cover over and conceal many of the actual incidents of the four days from June 15th to 18th. The co-operation of the two armies had resulted in one of the most glorious one of the most complete victories on record—a victory which became the starting-point of modern European politics. It was but natural, therefore, that Gneisenau, whose position gave him so much authority during the campaign, should also be glad to accept his share in the glory without saying much about his feelings at the time of the battle. From a variety of causes Wellington too had no great wish to discuss any vexed question concerning Waterloo or to make known the full truth regarding the events which led to it. He was anxious to avoid having anything said that might offend the Belgians as many of the Dutch-Belgian troops, they had served under Napoleon in famous wars before and were warmly attached to his interests, had not behaved well in this campaign against him. Moreover, many things had occurred in the British army that were not in accordance with Wellington's plans or intentions and he must have felt that some of his own proceedings were fairly open to hostile criticism. His movements had been slow and he had been mistaken in his conception of his great opponent's plan of operations. Indeed, he had been so deceived by Napoleon's cleverly devised movements that up to almost the last moment he persisted in believing that the French army would manœuvre round the English right in order to cut him off from his line of retreat upon Ostend. Besides, his staff had not served him well. Many of them had been foisted upon him from home by private and family interests and even against his wishes. Believing in their statements he had in the forenoon of June 15th, as will be mentioned later on, written Blucher a letter in which the positions occupied by his troops at the moment were incorrectly stated. Altogether he had abundant reasons for wishing his official account of the battle and of the operations which preceded it to be accepted as final and without question. In after years, whenever asked to help in preparing any work on the campaign, he usually answered with some degree of testiness that his despatch contained all that was necessary. He well knew that it contained many inaccuracies and, in fact, that no commander writing immediately after any great battle ever can know nearly all that has happened. In this particular instance there was an unusual number of mistakes in his despatch. He tells us in it, for example, that at Quatre Bras he was attacked, amongst other troops, by D'Erlon's corps which we know was not there at all. Very serious errors have also been introduced into the history of this campaign which have their sole origin in the untruthful statements dictated by Napoleon at St. Helena. Brilliant as were the Emperor's plans for 1815 and ably as he directed a great part of them, he yet made some very serious mistakes during their general execution. He was fully aware of this, and with his subtle Italian genius tried in his St. Helena writings to prove that everything he did was right, to conceal these mistakes from posterity and ungenerously to throw upon subordinates the responsibility for all that went wrong. So absolutely dishonest and misleading is his account of Waterloo that many of those who hate his memory and the system his name represents have unfairly used it in order the more effectively to decry and discredit all he ever said or wrote about his own wars.

As far as concerns the historical student the practical result of all these causes is that much of the published information upon which we have to rely has been seriously tainted at its source. Statement and counter-statement have followed one another in quick succession until the literature of this campaign alone forms quite a library in itself.

On the Anglo-Prussian side Müffling was the only man who, knowing the facts, attempted to give any account of what actually did take place between the two Allied commanders. But in summarising it he purposely slurred over much that was of importance. Yet he has been generally accepted as a final authority by English historians. To attempt therefore, to give such a brief account of the Waterloo story as is alone possible in these pages is to write with feelings somewhat akin to those of the man who has to dance amongst eggs. I shall, however, endeavour to avoid stating doubtful stories, though I cannot hope in this brief narrative to satisfy all those who have vehemently espoused some one side or another in the various controversies.

The French army with which Napoleon took the field in Belgium consisted of six army corps, one of which was the Imperial Guard. Three of them were very weak and none were strong. The Reserve Cavalry, four corps of 13,500 sabres in all, was under Grouchy. There was also a cavalry division with each of five out of the six army corps, so that the total force in this arm numbered about 22,000 sabres. The Infantry was about 85,000, making a fighting force of 344 guns and 107,000 sabres and bayonets, not including some ten thousand artillerymen and five or six thousand train and engineers ; let us say, an army of 344 guns and of about 123,000 men of all arms. As far as its numbers went, Napoleon had never commanded a finer body of well-trained and well-seasoned soldiers. All were Frenchmen inspired with the splendid fighting spirit of their nation, and, excepting perhaps a few of the superior officers, all devoted to Napoleon and believing that his cause was their cause and the cause of France. No men could have fought better than they did, and although Waterloo was the most disastrous defeat France had sustained since Blenheim she has every reason to be proud of the manner in which her sons fought on that memorable June Sunday.

The Prussian army under Blucher, which as well as the English army was largely composed of recruits and militiamen, was divided into four army corps. Unlike Wellington's army, however, it was a purely national force, intensely German in feeling and inflamed with a deadly hatred of the French and with a splendid feeling of intense patriotism. The first corps, under Ziethen, held Charleroi and the Sambre valley above it as far as the French frontier; the second, under

BLUCHER.

Pirch, was in and around Namur; the third, under Thielmann, was at Ciney and in its vicinity; and the fourth, under Bülow, was on the extreme left at Liége, nearly sixty miles from the extreme right near Charleroi. Each of these four army corps was scattered in widely extending cantonments and would require many hours of hard marching to concentrate before it could move upon any point of general assembly for the whole army. The total strength of this Prussian army may be reckoned at about 100,000 infantry, 11,800 cavalry, and 312 guns. Owing to the small proportion of well-trained regular soldiers in its ranks, its quality as a fighting force was much inferior to that of any Prussian army which had ever before taken the field against Napoleon.

Wellington's army consisted of two corps, a reserve, and a corps of cavalry. The gallant but inexperienced Prince of Orange commanded the first, which was distributed about Mons, Enghien and Nivelles in continuation westward of the Prussian line; the second, under Lord Hill, prolonged the line still further westward as far as the Scheldt. The English cavalry and that of the German Legion were under Lord Uxbridge. The Hanoverian, Brunswick and Netherlands cavalry were with the several contingents furnished by each country. In numbers, this motley army of many nations did not certainly exceed 80,000 foot, 14,000 horse, and about 9000 gunners, engineers, and train—say in all 94,000 sabres and bayonets, and 184 guns. There were twelve eighteen-pounders besides; but the Duke, for some unexplained reason, left them behind at Antwerp. How often he must have wished for them on June 18th, for they would have been of incalculable value many times that day! Of this army nearly 30,000 were Dutch and Belgian soldiers whose sympathies were largely with Napoleon, and only about 31,000 were British. The inferior quality of the soldiers composing it, the haste with which it had been so recently organised, and, with a few exceptions, the mediocrity of its subordinate general officers, all combined to make it what Wellington contemptuously pronounced it—"the worst army he had ever commanded." Its 14,000 horsemen compared unfavourably with Napoleon's magnificent body of 22,000 cavalry, though Blucher's 11,800 cavalry were of good stuff and well commanded.

From the foregoing statement it will be seen that the two Allied armies extended over a front of 100 miles from east to west, and covered a depth of about 40 miles from north to south. I think that any military critic of to-day who would defend this inordinate dispersion of Wellington's and Blucher's armies, especially of the former, must be blinded by national prejudices. Had the Duke been beaten at Waterloo history would surely have condemned the position of his army on June 13th, 14th and 15th, and also his decision to maintain it until the French attack had been fully developed instead of at once concentrating when he first learned that the enemy's columns had reached Maubeuge.

There can be little doubt that Wellington had been misled by his spies and other sources of secret information as to the forwardness of Napoleon's preparations, and that he did not consequently expect the French to enter Belgium before July 1st at earliest. But when he ascertained for certain that the enemy were collecting near Maubeuge it seems to have been unwise—to use a mild adjective—to have left his army in the scattered cantonments it then occupied. On the 13th each of the two Allied armies should have concentrated within supporting distance of each other. From the numbers I have given the reader will see that it was Napoleon's deliberate intention, with a concentrated army of about 22,000 sabres, 85,000 bayonets and 344 guns, to attack the armies of Blucher and Wellington, which, though very inferior in quality to his army, would if united make up a total force of 25,800 sabres, 180,000 bayonets and 496 guns. It must be remembered, however, that he knew the two Allied armies to be so scattered as to afford him every reason for hoping he would be able to deal with each separately; that he was also well aware of how inferior their soldiers were to his old and well-seasoned troops, and furthermore, that the fighting worth as well as the loyalty of some of their contingents was more than doubtful.

Napoleon's military instinct always favoured offensive operations in war. His defensive campaign of the previous year was carried on against the grain and he had no wish to repeat it. Besides, he was determined, if possible, to save France from all the horrors of another invasion. He believed that he could out-manœuvre Wellington and he was certain, from previous experience, that Blucher would be but a *child* in his hands. The calculation upon which he based his plan of campaign was briefly, that if he could obtain a brilliant success over these two generals —then so near his frontier—his returned fortune and the elation consequent upon victory would arouse an enthusiasm in France which would enable him to largely increase his army in the field and would rally the Belgians, the Dutch, and possibly others to his standard. It might also cause some of the armies then marching upon France to pause and might induce some to make peace, or at least it might sow dissension amongst the Allies and would surely gain him time to consolidate his power and increase his army.

Knowing that Wellington and Blucher together far exceeded the French army in strength, Napoleon's one chance of success lay in being able to fight them separately. The difficult nature of the country known as the Ardennes and the scantiness of the supplies to be found there made any attack upon the Allies' left practically impossible. His selection of a line of advance and the part of the enemy's line he would fall upon was consequently limited to a choice between attacking their right, which would bring him upon the English line of communication with the seacoast, or their centre—that is, the point of junction between the two armies. Wellington believed that his great opponent would try the first-mentioned alternative, and to the end of his days was of opinion that he ought to have done so. I cannot enter here into his many reasons for these conclusions, but most soldiers well-trained in the science of war would have then thought otherwise, and think so now. An attack upon the Allied right could not possibly have afforded Napoleon the same rapid and conclusive results that a severance of the Allied armies, by a successful attack upon the point where they joined, would have secured. Napoleon had accurate information as to the exact positions occupied by those armies, and it did not require his genius to perceive that the road from Charleroi to Brussels was practically the

L

dividing line between Blucher and Wellington. Charleroi, thirty-four miles by a very good road from the Belgian capital, was therefore his first objective point, and there and in its immediate neighbourhood he meant to cross the Sambre.

The tendency, as he well knew, of all Allied armies when so struck at is for each at once to look after its own line of communication and its own special safety. Blucher drew his supplies from a base on the Rhine; Wellington drew his from England *viâ* Ostend and Antwerp, which places constituted his base on the sea. Napoleon expected that the effect of his army suddenly crossing the Sambre near Charleroi to advance upon Brussels would be to cause each of the Allied armies to curl up, as it were, within itself, and so leave a gap between them into which he would be able to penetrate, and wedge-like to sever all communication between the two armies. This done, he did not anticipate any difficulty in destroying them one after the other. From all that he had heard of Wellington's operations in the Peninsula he counted upon his acting with great caution; and former experience of Blucher as an antagonist made him certain that the impetuous Prussian would rush wildly into the fray. He therefore counted upon being able to dispose of the Prussian army before the slowly and cautiously moving English could arrive to support it.

With Brussels in his possession he believed the Belgians would again throw in their lot with him and the Rhine would once more become his eastern frontier. The effect of this upon Europe would be great and might lead to the fall of the English ministry, which hated him, and their replacement by those unworthy men who were his friends, and who then clamoured loudly for peace at any price with France. The whole essence of Napoleon's plan was secrecy and celerity. His intentions to be successful must be carefully veiled from the enemy who must be thoroughly deceived until the moment when the sudden blow was to be struck. Fortunately for his enterprise the old line of Vauban's frontier fortresses between the Meuse and Dunkirk still existed, and they were in fair order. Their possession enabled him to conceal his doings and designs, and he could concentrate troops behind them without their being immediately discovered by the enemy. He was able also, by a skilful distribution of national guards along the open frontier near Mons, between the Sambre and the Scheldt, to make Wellington believe that the blow was about to fall on his right. It was this conviction of Wellington's which accounts for the want of cohesion between the Allied armies when the French troops had reached their appointed rendezvous immediately south of the Sambre on the evening of June 14th.

Napoleon left Paris for Charleroi on June 12th, well neither in body nor in mind. He was fully aware that he was not the man physically he had been at Marengo or at Austerlitz, and his mind was full of care. A firm believer in luck, all had gone so much against him during the three previous years that he scarcely dared to trust in fortune. "Ah," said he, "you do not know what a force good luck is! It alone imparts courage. It is the feeling that fortune is with us which gives us the hardihood to dare. Not to dare is to do nothing of moment, and one never dares except as the result of good luck. Misfortune depresses and blights the soul, and from thenceforward one does nothing good." A few days before he left Paris he told Davoust and the Count de Ségur —the elder—that he had no longer any confidence in his star, and his worn depressed look was in keeping with his words. We are told he was superstitious: how much therefore this feeling must have acted upon him! Indeed, he admitted that he "felt an abatement of spirit, and had an instinct of an unpropitious issue."

By a series of very cleverly devised movements, in the execution of which however his lieutenants made many mistakes, Napoleon brought his army together on the evening of June 14th within a short march of Charleroi. Gérard's corps* which formed the right of the line and was coming from the Moselle south of the Ardennes, had not yet quite reached Philippeville, its allotted place of rendezvous, owing to the badness of the roads; but the centre consisting of Vandamme's, Lobau's and the Guard Corps was at Beaumont, where Napoleon fixed his headquarters for the night; and the extreme left, made up of D'Erlon's and Reille's Corps which had been stationed on the open Belgian frontier, had reached Solre-sur-Sambre. All these three places of rendezvous were within French territory and were nearly equidistant, about fifteen

---

* The reader must not confuse General Gérard who commanded the 4th Corps, with General Girard who only commanded a Division (the 7th) in Reille's Corps (the 2nd).

miles, from Charleroi. His first object was to get his army across the Sambre and to seize Quatre Bras and Sombreffe—they were eight miles apart and both about thirteen miles beyond Charleroi—as their possession would give him the Namur-Nivelles road, the chief line of intercommunication between the two Allied armies. Quatre Bras was only twenty-one miles from Brussels.

The Prussian outposts soon detected the fact that a great army was being assembled in their neighbourhood, but they failed to discover the French right wing which, under Gérard, was so much nearer to Charleroi than to Mons that its discovery would certainly have indicated the fact that Charleroi and not Mons was the point aimed at. As it was, the French troops at Solre discovered by the Prussian cavalry were as near Mons in point of distance and nearer it in time of marching than they were to Charleroi. Now as Mons was held by the English, an attack in that direction would have implied the intention of assailing Wellington's army in the first instance before any attempt was made against Blucher. As already mentioned, the English general was so convinced that the attack would be made on his right that it was only with difficulty and very slowly that he brought his mind to realise how mistaken he was. At last, when it was nearly being too late, he perceived that it was the right of the Prussian line and the point of junction between it and the left of his own army which Napoleon aimed at.

The possibility of Napoleon advancing into Belgium by Charleroi and the bridges over the Sambre in its neighbourhood in order to sever and drive apart the two Allied armies, had been discussed by Wellington and Blucher as far back as the beginning of May. At this conference a plan of action to meet such a contingency was decided upon. The Prussian army was to concentrate between Sombreffe and Charleroi, and the English between Gosselies and the bridge at Marchiennes. This would bring the two Allied armies so close together that no attack upon one could be made by Napoleon without having the other on his flank. Yet, as a matter of fact, by 3 p.m. on the 15th only one Prussian corps was near the intended point of concentration, and of Wellington's army but one division was in the vicinity, although 40,000 French had already crossed the Sambre at Marchiennes and 70,000 more were then entering Charleroi. This is a circumstance which cannot be ignored by the worshippers of Wellington, for it clearly shows how indifferent were his arrangements for giving effect to a plan of such first importance and so maturely considered and deliberately adopted as this plan had been. The fact is, Wellington at Brussels was too far from the theatre of action: he ought to have been at Nivelles or still better at Quatre Bras all the 15th. Had he been at the latter place he would not certainly have allowed the day to pass without orders for the immediate concentration of his army there or in its neighbourhood. But throughout this first day Wellington does not seem to have realised the importance of Quatre Bras to his army.

Before any move had been made by the Allies to

oppose him, Napoleon was thus with his whole army within striking distance of Ziethen's single corps of only 32,000 men, and, from what he knew of the character of his two antagonists, he fully hoped to bring the bulk of his army into such a position as would enable him to crush Blucher before Wellington could support him, and perhaps even before the whole Prussian army had been concentrated.

Napoleon's orders were that his army should move to the attack on June 15th, at 3 a.m. But, unfortunately for him, Vandamme, whose corps lay in front of the central column, did not receive this order. Gérard's corps, on the right, was delayed both by the fact that his divisions had not been properly closed up the evening before and by the desertion on the march of General Bourmont who was leading the advance. Reille's corps, which led the left wing, moved off in good time, and D'Erlon followed slowly behind him.

Ziethen, in a most skilful manner, took good advantage of the opportunities which the French passage of the Sambre afforded him. He succeeded in not only seriously delaying the enemy's advance but in safely withdrawing his own corps in admirable order and with little loss considering the overwhelming force opposed to him and the ability of its leader. He made one serious mistake, however, in not destroying the bridges over the Sambre at Marchiennes, Charleroi and at Chatelet.

During the afternoon of this day, the 15th, Ney joined the Emperor near Charleroi, probably about 5 p.m. Having only received his orders at the last moment, he had hurried forward with no staff but one aide-de-camp. Napoleon at once assigned him the command of the left wing of the army, consisting of Reille's and D'Erlon's corps, and ordered him to push the enemy along the Quatre Bras road. Whether he did or did not order Ney to seize Quatre Bras that night is a much disputed point. At any rate, riding forward towards it at a brisk pace, Ney overtook the leading troops of his command at a moment when Reille, having already cleared the road of the retreating Prussians who fell back eastwards, was moving upon Gosselies.

Pushing on with Bachelu's division and Piré's cavalry Ney found the village of Frasnes occupied by Wellington's outposts, which upon his approach fell back towards Quatre Bras. Not being able in the darkness of the evening to make out the strength of the troops holding the last-named place, Ney restricted his operations for that day to the occupation of Frasnes by Bachelu's infantry and some cavalry in support. Of the remainder of Reille's corps, Girard's division was in pursuit of the Prussians who had, as already mentioned, gone off in an easterly direction, and its two remaining infantry divisions were still in rear of Gosselies. D'Erlon's corps, moving in rear of Reille, had been much more delayed—indeed part of it was still south of the Sambre. The small detachments of Wellington's army which the French had actually encountered had been moved backwards without the Duke's orders and contrary to his wishes, by their own commander Prince Bernhard of Saxe-Weimar. Though Napoleon was not yet aware of it

Blucher had ordered all his three other army corps to support that of Ziethen. Of these, Bülow's corps at Liége had been seriously delayed by a mistake in the nature of the orders sent to it.

It will thus be seen that what Napoleon wished and had calculated on had so far been realised: namely, that whilst Wellington's army had been very slow in its movements, Blucher, with his usual impetuosity, was hurrying forward with only three of his army corps to the very locality where Napoleon wished to fight him. Although, according to Napoleon's explicit orders, the whole of his army was to have been north of the Sambre before noon, some 35,000 French soldiers slept that night on the other side of that river. But on the whole, despite these and some other vexatious delays, Napoleon had good reason to be well satisfied with the result of the operations on June 15th.

Before noon of the following day, the 16th, three Prussian army corps were gathered on what is now known as the famous battlefield of Ligny, and about noon Blucher received a letter which Wellington had despatched at 10.30 a.m. from the heights north of Frasnes, that is, about a couple of miles south of Quatre Bras. This letter, unknown to the earlier historians of the campaign and only unearthed from the Prussian archives in 1876, has been since then the subject of much controversy both in Germany and in England. I have not space to discuss it here or even to give the contents in full. Suffice it to say that, as stated already, it mentioned the positions which the Duke then believed were occupied by his still widely disseminated army. It went on to give Prince Blucher every reason to hope that a large portion at least of the English army would be able to arrive in time to actually support the Prussians at Ligny. That if unable to do so, Wellington would at least effect so powerful a diversion in their favour that Napoleon would be unable to employ against them more than a moiety of his army. Wellington, an English gentleman of the highest type, was wholly and absolutely incapable of anything bordering on untruth or deceit in dealing with his Allies, and without any doubt whatever believed unqualifiedly in all that he stated in this letter. He must therefore have been misled by his inefficient staff in this matter.

Following his letter, the Duke at 1 p.m. had himself a conversation with Blucher. The nature of that conversation is very uncertain in many respects and its character is variously recorded by different writers. It is safer therefore to assume that both these leaders planned and acted under the impression that the statements contained in this letter were actually correct. Under that impression they arranged for the direction in which the English army should move to support Blucher at Ligny. Wellington either made a conditional promise to come to Blucher's aid provided he was not himself attacked, or he simply made arrangements for the intended movement. It is evident that at the time he supposed nearly the whole of the French army was being directed against the Prussians, for he had written from Frasnes that he saw few French troops in that direction. It is a noteworthy fact that having conferred with Blucher and examined his dispositions at Ligny and seen all he could of the French army there, he predicted Blucher's defeat.

Blucher had originally arranged for the concentration of his army in the neighbourhood of Sombreffe, but he had done so at a time when he fully expected he could assemble all his four army corps there in line of battle and when he counted also upon receiving considerable assistance from Wellington. This expectation of support was increased by the receipt of Wellington's letter about noon on the 16th. But it is simply preposterous to assert that Blucher fought at Ligny because of that letter or of any promise made to him by Wellington that day, no matter what may have passed between the two generals at Ligny, because when Wellington was there, at 1 p.m., the French columns were already actually advancing to the attack. Blucher's decision to fight must therefore have been arrived at long before.

Though the whole story of this letter has been sprung upon us lately, I dwell upon the question it raises because it is one that very closely concerns our national honour. The positions which Wellington's letter specified as then occupied by his troops had not been reached by all of them when he wrote it, and in several cases they were not reached for many hours later. In fact, there was no prospect whatever that Wellington could afford Blucher the support he hoped for at Ligny. Gneisenau, already suspicious of the English commander, was naturally affected in his after conduct of the campaign by the doubts of

Wellington's honesty occasioned by this letter and the Prussian defeat at Ligny. He carried to his grave the suspicion that our great Duke had deliberately deceived Prince Blucher in order to make him fight at Ligny so that the English army—unduly scattered—might have time to concentrate. The publication of Gneisenau's life, some years after the discovery of this important letter, gave rise for a time in some quarters of Germany to a bitter feeling on the subject. For my purpose here it is more important to note, as will be seen presently, that these circumstances nearly wrecked the prospects of the Allies by their influence on the mind of the man who at the moment practically directed the strategy of Blucher's army.

How it happened that Wellington was so misinformed of the actual points which his army had reached when he wrote this letter we can only conjecture. The orders he gave for the concentration of his army were probably sent out by his staff later than he supposed; the messengers who took those orders were certainly longer in delivering them than had been calculated upon; his staff—not of his own choosing—were probably disposed to take an optimistic view of the positions reached by the troops when they framed the statement for him upon the strength of which he wrote to Blucher.

It is interesting to turn from this discussion, where we have to grope about for probabilities without any certainty as to facts, to review the strange chain of chances which prevented Napoleon from gaining the full or even anything approaching the full benefit from the position he had gained for his army on the 15th. He had succeeded beyond all reasonable expectations in placing it where he was able to deal with Blucher whilst one-fourth of the Prussian force was distant and beyond all chance of taking part in the battle and before Wellington could support his Ally.

In the first place the French army had not closed up to its front by the evening of the 15th, as ordered by Napoleon. Without doubt the men were somewhat overdone by their immense exertions of the few previous days and they wanted rest. But the delay on the part of D'Erlon, who had been ordered to close on Reille's Corps, is unaccountable, and it is hardly possible to excuse that general for it, even though his troops were weary and had to work over bad roads much cut up by the corps immediately in front of them. On the other hand all experienced soldiers are well aware of the delays inseparable from marches undertaken under these circumstances.

Ney, who was in command of both Reille's and D'Erlon's army corps, had spent about an hour and a half on the evening of the 15th with Napoleon at Charleroi, and returned to Gosselies about 2 a.m. on the 16th without any positive orders from the Emperor for that day's operations. During the early morning those French who had bivouacked south of the Sambre crossed that river at Charleroi and Chatelet. At 8 a.m. on the 16th Soult, the Chief of the Imperial Staff, informed Ney that Kellerman's corps of cavalry had been ordered to join his command and at the same time asked him for news as to whether D'Erlon's corps had yet closed up, and what was the position of D'Erlon and of Reille, and also of the enemy.

Napoleon was far from well at this time. When he returned from the front to Charleroi on the evening of the 15th he was overwhelmed with fatigue and threw himself on his bed exhausted. On the following

SOULT.

morning, when every moment of daylight was of the utmost consequence, we have it on good authority that he was prostrated with languor and unable to attend to any business. It was daylight on June 16th shortly after 3 a.m., but yet no movement in advance was made until near 11 a.m. Between seven and eight hours were thus lost to Napoleon during which

Blucher was enabled to perfect his arrangements for the coming battle at Ligny. The two French wings were each waiting for the other to move. Napoleon, not very correctly informed as to the possible strength of the Prussians, and whom as late as about 8 or 9 o'clock a.m. he estimated at only 40,000 men, was anxious to have Ney's troops well forward on the Quatre Bras road, and to get his own columns, designed for an attack on Blucher, well closed up before they engaged. He informed Ney that as soon as he had brushed aside the Prussians then before him he would march to join Ney with the Reserve and push on with him to Brussels. Ney, however, and Reille also held back for some time owing to the reports they received from Girard, who had been watching the Prussians all the morning as they formed for battle near Ligny. The movements of the French Left on the Charleroi-Brussels road were consequently slower than Napoleon had a right to expect, so that it was not until 2 p.m. that Ney, with only two out of the four divisions of Reille's corps and Piré's cavalry, assailed the Dutch-Belgian troops at Quatre Bras. Prince Jerome's division did not arrive until an hour later, and Girard's division, engaged in watching the Prussians, as already stated, became eventually involved in the battle of Ligny. This appears to have been entirely the result of Ney's and Reille's action, as they wished to retain Girard near the Prussians to protect their own right flank during their advance upon Quatre Bras.

Had Napoleon set his troops in motion at 5 or even 6 a.m. on the 16th, the result of the day's fighting must have been very different. At a time when every hour was worth a reinforcement of 10,000 men, he allowed at least seven hours of daylight to

JEROME.

slip by to little purpose. As it was, this delay gave Wellington time to reach Quatre Bras again about 2.30 p.m., and before the Dutch-Belgian division there had been completely crushed by the superior numbers and especially by the better fighting quality of the French soldiers engaged. About an hour later Picton's division arrived, and from that time on successive reinforcements of English troops came up. This gave Wellington a continuously increasing advantage over the cavalry and three unsupported divisions of Reille's corps, then in action, until at last he was able in the evening to assume the offensive and drive Ney back. Strange occurrences had deprived not only Ney but both wings of the French army of any help from D'Erlon whose corps all through the day seemed to have worked only mischief for Napoleon.

The corps of Vandamme and Gérard had been assigned to Grouchy, just as those of Reille and D'Erlon had been placed under Ney's command. Early in the morning Napoleon ordered Grouchy to attack the Prussians in front of him, intending, for the day at least, to support him with the remainder of the army which he held in his own hands as a Reserve. As soon as the Prussians had been crushed it was Napoleon's intention to transfer that Reserve to his left wing and then force his own way to Brussels.

About 2 p.m. Napoleon sent an order to Ney directing him, with the corps of D'Erlon and Reille and the cavalry attached to him, to drive the English from Quatre Bras and then sweep round in rear of the Prussians whilst Grouchy attacked them in front at 2.30 p.m. When at 3.15 p.m. the strength of the Prussian army had become more evident this order

M

was reiterated. Upon reaching the headquarters of D'Erlon's corps, as it was approaching Frasnes, the aide-de-camp who carried this last-mentioned despatch took upon himself the responsibility of turning it off at once towards the right wing, thus completely misinterpreting the nature of Napoleon's order and sending D'Erlon and his corps into a false position as regarded the general scheme of advance. About 6.30 p.m. D'Erlon's corps reached the outskirts of the field of Ligny to the serious alarm of Vandamme who took it to be a portion of Wellington's army that had somehow broken through the French line and was about to fall on his rear. He reported this to Napoleon. The moment was critical for the Emperor was in the act of preparing for the final attack of his Guard upon the Prussians. This alarm compelled him to postpone the attack, and it was not until 7.30 p.m., when he had obtained correct information, that he ordered the movement to be resumed. Thus another precious hour of daylight was lost. In the meantime Ney, horrified at the absence of the very troops that had been placed at his disposal to carry out Napoleon's plan of attack, despatched a peremptory order to D'Erlon to return forthwith. This order only reached D'Erlon as he was deploying to take part in the battle then raging at Ligny. His men were tired after their long day's march and it took a long time to reform column of route and join Marshal Ney. It was late in the evening when he did so and not until Wellington had had time to defeat Ney who had done his best to effect with three divisions what Napoleon intended he should have attempted with eight. This is a good illustration of the mishaps which abound in war.

Before night fell Napoleon had broken the Prussian centre and, driving the wings apart had gained a complete but by no means a crushing victory at Ligny. It is obvious that the whole character of the results of the day's operations had been changed by the loss of the services of D'Erlon's corps and by the misuse of Girard's division. So late were all Wellington's arrangements for the concentration of his army that had Ney's two corps been concentrated as early as Napoleon intended, and as they well might have been, they could easily have seized Quatre Bras and brushed aside the few Allied troops that were then alone available in that quarter. How certain this is may be estimated from the fact that the Duke in his official report states that he was attacked at Quatre Bras by the whole of both D'Erlon's and Reille's two corps—that is by nearer three times than twice as many infantry as he was actually engaged with. Had D'Erlon and Girard been with Ney early in the day Wellington must have been driven away from Quatre Bras by 4 or 5 p.m. D'Erlon would then have had time to have arrived by the main road in the rear of Blucher just as he was receiving his final blow from Napoleon in the gloaming of the evening. Had all this taken place as Napoleon intended it is hardly too much to say that both Ziethen's and Pirck's corps, which formed Blucher's right wing, must have been destroyed and in all probability the headquarters staff, including Prince Blucher and General Gneisenau, would have been captured. As it was, the following morning Thielmann told Bülow that he believed it was Blucher's intention to make for the Rhine *viâ* St. Trond. Had this retreat been decided on there would have been no Battle of Waterloo, for certainly Wellington would not have fought there without a positive promise of Prussian support. He would have fallen back upon the coast abandoning Brussels to its fate. Had this been the result of Ligny the campaign might have ended in glorious triumph for Napoleon; from that misfortune Europe was saved by the heroic public spirit of Prince Blucher, the most patriotic, noble and chivalrous of gallant soldiers.

In the final charge Blucher was unhorsed, wounded, and supposed to have been taken prisoner. For the moment the command devolved on Gneisenau, his chief of the staff. Standing on a hillock surrounded by the generals and staff of the only two corps with which he could communicate for the moment, Gneisenau gave what became the decisive order of the campaign. He ordered the retreat upon Wavre, thereby abandoning his direct lines of communication through both Namur and Liége. Until recently it was always assumed that in giving this order he designed to prepare the way for that junction with Wellington which two days afterwards decided the issue of the campaign. His late biographer, however, has made it known that his original order was for a retreat on Tilly which he subsequently changed to Wavre when he found that Tilly was not marked on their working maps. It would therefore seem that

Wavre was named as the general direction, that is northwards, which the retreating columns were to take. In fact, in no other direction could he hope to safely reunite the two separated wings of the Prussian army. Moreover, in moving upon Wavre he did not abandon his possible retreat on the Rhine, for, as a matter of fact he did at once re-establish his main line of communications with his base through St. Trond on Maestricht. The retreat of the two corps, those of Thielmann and Bülow, then with the Prussian headquarters was carried that evening just far enough to relieve them for the time of all pressure from the French. The following morning all the four Prussian corps resumed their march towards Wavre and so ended the battle of Ligny.

Napoleon's plan for the battle of Ligny was quite in his best style but the mode in which it was executed was unworthy of his reputation. He must be held responsible for the delays which so long deferred the opening attack and which subsequently postponed the final blow until darkness had set in. Some of those who are dazzled by the "Napoleonic Legend" may possibly traverse this conclusion, but few indeed can hold him blameless for having failed to follow up the defeated Prussians at once in order to complete their rout. Instead of pursuing them with every available man he allowed them to effect their retreat without molestation. Grouchy, though a very second-rate commander, wished to follow them; but, as Napoleon, who had left the field without issuing any orders, was ill and asleep at Fleuras and as no one dared to waken him this much-abused marshal could do nothing. The object of the battle was to completely overwhelm Blucher and prevent his junction with Wellington. But Napoleon by abandoning all pursuit of the Prussians when he had defeated them failed to reap that great object from the battle.

## CHAPTER VI.

### WATERLOO.

EARLY in the morning of June 17th, Wellington, who had gone back to sleep at Genappe after his success at Quatre Bras, rode to the field of his previous day's battle. The Prussian messenger sent to inform him of Blucher's defeat had been wounded, so he first learnt the news from his own staff. Upon his arrival at Quatre Bras, finding that there was no serious movement on the part of the French in that direction, he made dispositions to fall back at his own leisure and when he deemed it necessary to do so. At 9 a.m. an officer from Blucher arrived to tell him that the Prussian army was gathering at Wavre. In reply Wellington said he would stand and fight south of the forest of Soignes, near Mont St. Jean, if Blucher would support him by one, or as some accounts have it, by two Prussian Army Corps. It was not until late at night that Blucher was in a position to send Wellington an answer, for the Prussian artillery trains only reached Wavre at 5 p.m. and it was not until 11.30 p.m. that Bülow reported the arrival of his corps at Diont le Mont. It was not, therefore, until after that hour and after Müffling had reported to Blucher that the English army was in position at Mont St. Jean, that Blucher sent Wellington the assurance of Prussian support. Blucher's despatch assured Wellington that Bülow's corps would march at daybreak for St. Lambert, that Pirch's corps would support Bülow and that the other two corps would be held in readiness to move. At what hour this despatch reached Müffling we do not know, but as the bearer of it must have travelled by night over ten miles of bad road, its contents can hardly have been communicated to the Duke much before 3 a.m. on the 18th. As for Napoleon, he was so prostrated from the exertions of the day that he went to bed as soon as the battle of Ligny was over and was in such an exhausted condition that no one would venture on rousing him to ask for orders. The next morning it was the same: he could not be roused to active work at this critical moment when rapid decision was essential to success.

The morning of the 17th was passed in inactivity by both wings of the French army. Pajol indeed, with a force of light cavalry, had started early, in pursuit of Blucher, but as he took the road to Namur and made some chance and deceptive captures on it, his reports only tended to mislead the Emperor as to the direction of the Prussian retreat. Ney, by some strange carelessness, had not been informed of the result of the battle of Ligny. He was thoroughly out of humour because he had been deprived of D'Erlon's corps on the previous day, and he made no attempt to beat up the English at Quatre Bras. Napoleon, apparently

THE FIELD OF WATERLOO.

taking for granted that the English must now retreat, spent the morning in talking politics. Some time was of course required to reorganise the regiments that had been engaged, and to refill the men's cartouches and the artillery ammunition waggons. But Napoleon allowed the delays to run on till midday, at which hour he at last despatched Grouchy, with the corps of Vandamme and Gérard and the cavalry of Pajol and Excelmans, in pursuit of the Prussians by the Gembloux road. It was not until 2 p.m. that Grouchy was able to march, and when he did, torrents of rain so impeded the movement that he did not reach Gembloux until late in the evening. Though fit to command a Division in action he was quite unequal to the task now imposed upon him. The verbal orders he received from Napoleon were to overtake the retreating Prussians and keep them in view wherever they went. At this time all the evidence pointed to Namur as the direction of their retreat. These orders were hardly spoken when reports from his cavalry informed the Emperor that at 9 a.m. a force of some 20,000 Prussians had been seen at Gembloux. He accordingly sent a written order to Grouchy desiring him from Gembloux to explore in the Namur and Maestricht direction. He added however these words: "It is important to penetrate what the enemy intend to do: whether they are separating themselves from the English, or whether they still intend to unite in order to cover Brussels and Liége trying the chances of another battle." It will be seen that he gave Grouchy no instructions to interpose in any event between him and the Prussians. To complete first the story of Grouchy for the 17th: upon reaching Gembloux he ascertained that some of the Prussians had taken the road to Wavre and some were, as he thought, moving on Maestricht. In reporting his proceedings to Napoleon he said: "If the mass of the Prussians is retiring on Wavre I shall follow in that direction in order to prevent them reaching Brussels and in order to separate them from Wellington." In accordance with this intention he issued orders for the movement on Wavre the following day, the memorable June 18th. When Napoleon had issued his orders to Grouchy on the 17th he at once started for Marbais with the Guard, Lobau's Corps and the Reserve Cavalry, in order to support Ney's attack upon the English at Quatre Bras. During the morning he had repeatedly ordered Ney to make this attack; but, perhaps from ill-temper about his defeat the previous day, that general made no movement until 1 p.m., when he saw Napoleon approaching. The force collected by Wellington at Quatre Bras, amounting to 45,000 men, began to fall back on Mont St. Jean about 10 a.m. on the 17th. The movement was leisurely and admirably carried out under the Duke's personal direction, and by the time that Ney actually began to move against him Wellington's cavalry alone remained on the position. By 2 p.m. the pursuit was retarded by the same torrential rain that had burst upon Grouchy's columns as he was setting out for Gembloux. With the exception of an insignificant skirmish at Genappe and such artillery fire as the French could bring to bear upon our retreating cavalry, nothing of interest marked this movement upon Mont St. Jean. Save for a detachment of 18,000 men, whom the Duke kept at Hal, being still anxious about his right, all

WELLINGTON.

his army was at last concentrated on what was to become the glorious battle-ground of the morrow. The French, toiling along over heavy, muddy roads during the evening and night of the 17th, did not get fully into position until very late that night or early the next morning.

As already stated, it is certain that Wellington had no intention of accepting battle on the 18th unless he was quite sure of Prussian assistance. On the other hand, we now know that he cannot have received any letter giving him a specific promise of such support until about 3 a.m. that morning—that is to say, at an hour when, if he meant to retreat, his arrangements for that operation ought to have been begun. It is difficult to understand his action according to the current history, but reports of conversations attributed to the Duke of Wellington in after years, from more than one quarter, have given rise to the following story: that late in the evening of the 17th he rode over to see Blucher and satisfied himself of the Prince's ability and intention to support him if he stood to fight on the 18th south of the forest of Soignes. The latest American historian of these events, Mr. Ropes in his very careful book, and using materials published by Colonel Maurice in his intensely interesting articles on Waterloo in the *United Service Magazine*, declares his belief in the story of this ride. There is no doubt that it would explain many things which it is otherwise difficult to understand. I am not, however, myself prepared to adopt it without some further proof, although, on the whole, the balance of evidence seems rather in its favour. As further evidence for or against it ought to be somewhere in existence, it would be a great service to historical truth as regards this ever interesting campaign, if those who could throw light on the matter would publish what they know.

In any case, by 10 a.m. of the 18th instant the head of Bülow's corps had reached St. Lambert and Wellington was aware of the fact. The whole of his corps did not however reach that village until the battle of Waterloo was far advanced. But Wellington did not know that Gneisenau, full of anxiety for the position in which the Prussian army would be if the English retreated and Blucher were to find Napoleon in front whilst Grouchy attacked him in rear, had ordered Bülow not to advance beyond St. Lambert until it was quite evident that Wellington meant really to fight it out at Waterloo and that the battle was fairly engaged. Whilst this storm was gathering on his flank Napoleon allowed himself to be delayed in making his attack upon the English army by the state of the ground which made all movements difficult, especially for artillery. At 10 a.m. he sent off a letter to Grouchy approving of his movement on Wavre "in order to approach us." The fact is that at this time neither Napoleon nor Grouchy dreamed of Blucher's bold and public-spirited movement, with all its risks, from Wavre to Waterloo. Their only dream of a junction by the Prussians with Wellington's army was in the direction of Brussels. On the other hand, in the original orders sent to Grouchy he had been directed to post detachments of cavalry to keep up communication with headquarters, and General Marbot tells us in his delightful memoirs that by Napoleon's orders he had established cavalry connection between the Imperial headquarters and the Dyle at Mouster and Ottignies. Had Grouchy carried out his orders on this point, his messengers must have encountered Marbot's horsemen at those villages. It was not till 1 p.m. that Napoleon received information of Bülow's arrival at St. Lambert with the head of his column; seeing that an attack upon his right flank was thus imminent, he sent at once to tell Grouchy, but the news reached that officer too late to affect his movements.

Before this, about 11.30 a.m., Napoleon had ordered the great battle to begin on which he must have felt his whole future depended. He directed Reille with his corps to attack Hougoumont as a diversion to his principle attack by D'Erlon's corps upon Wellington's left centre and centre at the village of Mont St. Jean.

The forces now standing face to face were not very unequal numerically except in guns. After his losses at Ligny and Quatre Bras, and without Grouchy whom he had detached to look after the Prussians, Napoleon was still able to bring into this new field of battle nearly 49,000 foot, 15,700 horse, and 246 guns. On the other hand, not counting the detachment of 18,000 men at Hal, Wellington had at Waterloo over 49,000 foot, 12,000 horse and 156 guns. Of the infantry, however, only 15,000 were English, and of the cavalry not quite half. His motley heterogeneous army was no more by itself a match for the French army in front of it in Wellington's judgment than it was in that of Napoleon.

The battle of Waterloo, as a detailed study of war, can only be described in greater space than I can here afford it. On the whole the facts concerning its many stirring episodes and heroic phases are much better known and more clearly established than they are about the other matters on which I have touched. I can only attempt to briefly summarise them here.

Reille's attack upon Hougoumont was badly executed, and he wasted the full strength of his corps upon it during nearly the whole day. To prepare the main attack by D'Erlon upon Wellington's centre Napoleon, out of his proportionately immense strength in artillery, pushed forward a battery of 78 guns within 600 yards of the crest-line of the English position. Up to 1.30 p.m. their fire was maintained without any reply from Wellington, his artillery being expressly ordered not to fire on the French batteries, but only on their columns as they advanced to the attack. The greater part of the British foot were well screened by the nature of the ground; but Bylandt's Dutch-Belgian Brigade was in front of the crest and much exposed. When D'Erlon's corps advanced in four huge columns, with the left thrown forward, this brigade fairly bolted. But when this unwieldy mass of French reached the crest it was utterly unable to deploy under the withering fire of artillery and small arms with which it was received. Charged with the bayonet by Picton's division whilst it was in hopeless confusion, and finally by Ponsonby's and Somerset's cavalry, it was sent reeling back with the loss of two eagles and numerous prisoners. The English horsemen pressing on their success too far were roughly handled. About 3 p.m., when D'Erlon's corps was thus severely shaken and whilst Reille was still busily occupied with trying to capture Hougoumont and Lobau's corps, with which Napoleon had meant to support Reille, had been turned off eastward to oppose the advancing Prussians, Ney sent to ask the Emperor for the support of a cavalry division. From the French lines at this time it looked as if the whole of the English position had been abandoned, for all Wellington's troops had quietly fallen back to their former stations behind the crest-line. To the French cavalry it seemed as if they had only to push forward and reap the fruits of a victory already won. When, therefore, this small body of cavalry, demanded by Ney, moved to the front the whole of the remaining French cavalry also dashed forward, either misunderstanding Napoleon's orders or without any orders at all; but in any case the movement was unchecked by the Emperor who was probably at the moment absorbed by the danger then threatening his right. How the splendid courage and wild career of these French horsemen broke upon the English squares is a well-known, an oft-told story. Not only one cavalry division but four were thus shattered. Nevertheless the infantry and artillery fire told severely upon these British squares during the intervals between the cavalry charges. As the day wore on Napoleon found himself obliged to support Lobau in his endeavours to keep back the Prussians, first with the Young Guard and then with three more battalions, and with five batteries in all. Before 7 p.m. these had cleared the Prussians out of Planchenoit which had been taken from Lobau an hour before. As soon as Napoleon had quite satisfied himself that the Prussian attack on his right flank had been repulsed and believing, as his previous information had given him to understand that this attack had been made by Bülow's corps only, he turned to again direct the battle against Wellington.

There is much discrepancy as to the hour when La Haye Sainte was captured. General Kennedy on the English side and Colonel Heymès, Ney's aide-de-camp, on that of the French put the hour at 6 p.m.—that is, towards the end of the period of the French cavalry charges. Others put it as early as 4 p.m. There is, however, one piece of evidence about which there can be little dispute: it is the copy of a letter from Lieutenant Græme of the Hanoverian service who took part in the defence of that place, a letter which has appeared in Siborne's recently published "Waterloo Letters" (p. 409). In it he mentions that when he was retreating from La Haye Sainte "all the army was formed in squares." It is clear, therefore, that the place fell during the period of the cavalry charges. The whole story of the defence and its details shows that it must have been towards evening that the French carried it. Owing to the length of the struggle for its possession and the neglect to provide a postern, the defenders were at last left without any ammunition. The denseness of the fog and smoke prevented any but those who were on the spot from seeing what was going on there; and, taking all the evidence we have on this point I am led to think that 6 p.m. must have been about the hour when La Haye Sainte fell. In fact the French took advantage of the circumstance that their cavalry were at the moment occupying the attention of Wellington and his army to renew and push home their direct attack upon this rather isolated outpost. Having once carried it they filled it with sharp-shooters. These made a neighbouring knoll untenable and enabled the French artillery to bring so heavy a fire upon a portion of the English position as to compel a square, composed of the 30th and 73rd regiments, to withdraw to a bank in rear, more or less in confusion. At the same moment some Brunswickers near this spot were driven back, and the consequence was a dangerous gap in the line of battle. It was a critical moment and if fresh French troops could have been immediately thrown into the gap it is practically certain that the English front must have been broken. Wellington met the danger with admirable coolness and skill. The arrival just at this juncture of one of Ziethen's brigades on his left released Vivian's and Vandeleur's brigades of horsemen and they were at once thrown into the gap. By the time that Napoleon was able to turn his attention from the Prussian attack at Planchenoit to this final attack upon the British who stood between him and Brussels, Wellington had thoroughly reformed his fighting line and Ziethen was within close supporting distance of him, while Pirch was closing up in support of Bülow for a renewed attack on Napoleon's right.

It was under these circumstances that the final attack by the Imperial Guard was made. It was preceded by a vigorous attack from two of D'Erlon's divisions on the English left which attack was maintained as long as the Guard attack continued. Only eight out of the twenty-four battalions of which the Guard consisted had been available for this final effort. Each attacking battalion was in a column of double companies and the whole advanced in echelon from the right. They moved diagonally across the front towards Wellington's right centre, and as they neared the British line they appear to have broken into two masses. The mass on the French right was received with a tremendous volley from the English Guards under Lord Saltoun and then charged. The leading French battalion, at least, was driven back in confusion and pursued; but the effect of this check to the leading column of the echelon was to bring up the other columns nearly into line with it. Saltoun's Guards, therefore, finding themselves for the moment threatened in flank by this seemingly fresh body, fell back to their old position. But as this new column advanced it in turn lent a flank to Adams' brigade, to which the 52nd—now the Oxfordshire Light Infantry under Colborne (Lord Seaton) belonged. Seizing the opportunity that able soldier poured in a tremendous volley at close range into the flank of the Imperial Guard. The column halted and endeavoured to front this unexpected attack, but Colborne, supported by the remainder of Adams' Brigade, charged the French whilst still in confusion, and the result was a complete rout. Wellington at once sent the cavalry brigades of Vivian and Vandeleur in pursuit. Almost at the same moment the main body of Ziethen's corps arrived, forcing itself in between the right of D'Erlon in his attack on the English left and the left of Lobau's corps in its contest with the

Prussians under Bülow. Ziethen thus turned both those French corps. The Duke seized the moment to order the general advance of his whole line. Despite the heroic efforts made by many splendid French soldiers, the rout soon became a mere *sauve qui peut*.

Whilst Napoleon's destruction was thus being accomplished at Waterloo, Grouchy had become involved in a simple rearguard action with Theilmann at Wavre. At a spot which has been very skilfully identified by Mr. Ropes as a certain house in Sartles-Walhains, Grouchy, when at breakfast, first heard the cannonade at Waterloo. He was urged by Gérard and Vandamme to march towards the battle which the sound indicated to be taking place near Planchenoit. But still hoping that by the occupation of Wavre he would be able to prevent the Prussians from joining Wellington, Grouchy determined to carry out his orders from Napoleon and push on for that place. The result of that decision was disastrous to Napoleon, as Grouchy's whole force, amounting to over 30,000 men with ninety-six guns, was throughout this eventful day as entirely useless to Napoleon as if it had not existed. M. Thiers, with the excessive and unscrupulous partisanship which characterises his Napoleonic epic, most unfairly throws upon Grouchy the blame for the final overthrow of his hero. Space does not allow me to enlarge upon this interesting and much disputed point. Mr. Ropes urges very forcibly that the words I have already quoted from Soult's written order of the 17th left Grouchy properly no choice but to march on the 18th by the bridges of Mouster and Ottignies to join Napoleon. This is, however, to assume that the Prussian move to join Wellington, as it was actually made, was one that might and ought fairly to have been anticipated by a rather commonplace general. But as a matter of fact, until 1 p.m. on the 18th there is nothing to show that Napoleon himself anticipated any such move on the part of Blucher. Even at that hour he thought it was only Bülow's corps that had marched against his right. No one can be better aware, no one can be prouder than I am, of the magnificent courage and steadiness of the British soldier at Waterloo; but when every allowance is made for it the honest historian must admit that it was the splendid audacity of this Prussian move upon St. Lambert and the French right, due to the personal loyalty of Prince Blucher to Wellington and in opposition to the strategic views of Gneisenau, that determined the fate of Napoleon's army at Waterloo. It is certain that Napoleon for the greater part of the 18th did expect Grouchy to march upon those bridges over the River Lasnes, but it was a move that only a far greater soldier than Grouchy and one ready to incur a vast responsibility, would have ventured upon. According to our present knowledge of the real position there can be no doubt that Grouchy ought to have disregarded his orders and moved with all speed towards the sound of the guns. By doing so he might have so occupied the Prussians as to gain for his master sufficient time to achieve a victory at Waterloo.

But it was not to be so. The French army was so hopelessly beaten and Wellington's victory was so complete that it was beyond even Napoleon's powers to recover from it. Grouchy indeed successfully led back into France the force under his command, but there was no army existing there that could hope to meet the host of invaders then ready to pour in over her frontiers. How Napoleon at length surrendered himself as a fugitive on board an English man-of-war and was ultimately deported to the beautiful and healthy Island of St. Helena, where he died nearly six years afterwards, is familiar to every English child.

Looking back now over the eventful period of "the hundred days," we are struck by the same features we have remarked in the previous campaigns I have here discussed. Was ever a man's personal ascendency more wonderfully displayed than it was by the fact that Napoleon, who disembarked in France almost alone and as a fugitive from his little island realm, was able in a few weeks to overturn without shedding blood the whole organised power of France under its legitimate king? But all throughout this his last campaign the ascendency he exercised over the Allies, compelling them to conform to his initiative, is not less remarkable than the narrowness by which he missed crushing them. What would have been the end of this extraordinary man had not D'Erlon's corps been wasted as it was on June 16th? With a little more vigour in the French cavalry reconnaissances of the 17th, what would have been the fate of the Prussian army if Napoleon had at once discovered its actual situation? I do not see how any one who closely follows the story of this four days' campaign, as it is now known to us, can doubt that

Ney, D'Erlon, Grouchy, and several others of Napoleon's subordinates failed to serve their old master with the vigour and enthusiastic zeal of former years. They as well as Europe generally were alike weary of him. But as to himself, suffering as he certainly was both in mind and body and by no means in any way the man to command victory as he had done in his early career, it is still round him and his initiative we find centred all that was most brilliant on the French side in this campaign. And yet there can be now no doubt that over him was cast a weariness and a lethargy, the result of ill-health, which weakened him and exercised an unfortunate spell over his actions.

Had Napoleon never made this bold attempt to seize again the throne of France, something would have been wanting to the dramatic interest and completeness of his fall. Nevertheless this Waterloo campaign is a thing apart, for Napoleon had in reality fallen before it began. As said by his eulogistic historian M. Thiers, who will see no fault in him as a general, his reign, attempted despite France as much as despite Europe, had become for the future impossible even before the campaign began.

To the preachers of Napoleonism, the final failure and overthrow of their idol was the result of a malignant destiny which influenced the elements as well as it did the conduct of subordinates who had formerly been his able assistants. They base their conclusions upon the statements, absolutely untruthful on some of the most important points, dictated by Napoleon at St. Helena. His narrative of the events of this campaign is admirable as a romance; its one great object was to make the world believe the lie which runs through it—I mean that he was himself infallible as a leader and in no way responsible for that terrible defeat the very name of which still rankles in the breast of Frenchmen. As far as France was concerned he was successful in this object; even so famous a national historian as M. Thiers has lent his great literary power to flatter the national vanity of his countrymen by throwing the blame of Napoleon's failure upon Grouchy, and in so doing has rendered that untruth immortal. At this moment the story of Waterloo as told by Thiers is firmly believed in by the great bulk of the French nation, and it is rare to find a Frenchman, no matter how anti-Napoleonic or how republican he may be in feeling, who does not believe that Waterloo was lost because Grouchy failed or refused to obey orders. Indeed, many of the uneducated still believe that he was bribed by England to play the traitor's part towards his old master. And so has been written in France the history of even the early part of this century!

The military critic who minutely examines Napoleon's proceedings during this campaign discovers so much to find fault with that it is only possible to account for his shortcomings by believing that they were due to the mysteriously recurring malady referred to already several times in these pages. The evidence corroborating this view is, to my mind, irrefutable. This disease, from which he had long suffered more or less and which had been the cause of so much disaster to him both in Russia and at the battle of Dresden, now attacked him oftener and with greater virulence. When under its influence he was incapable of all useful mental or bodily exertion, had great difficulty in keeping awake, and his drawn features and dull expression bespoke both physical pain and mental depression. His strength, no longer what it was ten years before, had been seriously overstrained by fifteen hours of daily work and worry during his anxious stay in Paris. But when not under the influence of this disease his fine intellect was as clear, his fertility of resource as marvellous, his genius as brilliant and his conceptions as grand as ever. Seated in his cabinet he could plan and devise as of yore, with almost unerring wisdom and keen appreciation of what was necessary for success. He could still grasp the position with all his former insight. But the anguish of his late failures in the field had not only seriously affected his health but had robbed him largely of that self-confidence which is so necessary for any great and continued success in war. He was no longer the thin, sleek, active little man he had been at Rivoli. His now bloated face, large stomach and fat and rounded legs bespoke a man unfitted for hard work on horseback. His unwieldy body no longer obeyed his behests as formerly. He was already old for his forty-seven years, and from being the most self-contained self-reliant and peremptory of leaders he had now to some marked extent already fallen into the garrulity of the greybeard, and was prone to ask opinions from those to whom he had been wont to issue orders.

I have thus dwelt upon the state of Napoleon's health in what I may term the last act of his curiously histrionic career, because I believe it to have been the primary cause of his final overthrow at Waterloo. The more I study his grandly conceived plan of campaign for 1815 the more convinced I am that the overwhelming defeat in which it ended was primarily the result of bodily disease and the failure of mental power which resulted from it at supreme moments when rapid and energetic decision was imperatively necessary for success. Had he been able to bring the mental and bodily energy of his early career to bear upon the great plan he had conceived for the destruction of Wellington and Blucher in Belgium, judging of what those commanders would have done by what they did do, I believe the cautious Englishman would at least have had to retreat in haste for the purpose of re-embarking at Ostend, whilst the fiery and impetuous Prussian would have been almost destroyed at Ligny and only too glad to place the Rhine between the remnants of his beaten army and the victor of Jena.

In no other way can I satisfactorily account for the valuable hours squandered by Napoleon or the careless faultiness of many of his most important orders during this campaign. Nor can I otherwise explain to myself how two armies situated as were those of Wellington and Blucher on June 14th 15th and 16th were allowed to escape during the two following days from the destruction with which Napoleon's most ably devised scheme of operations ought to have overwhelmed them. His fatigued and lethargic condition on the early morning of the 17th accounts for the many hours of daylight that were trifled away and were then uselessly squandered. Grouchy, anxious to begin the pursuit, strove to see Napoleon at daybreak, but was not admitted to his presence until 8 a.m., and even then it was impossible to elicit any definite instructions from him. Indeed, as a matter of fact, no orders were issued until noon, Grouchy receiving his verbally about 1 p.m.—a delay which enabled Blucher to reach Waterloo in time the following day to give the French their final despatch there. Well indeed may Vandamme have said to those around him: "The Napoleon whom we have known exists no more,—our yesterday's (the 16th) success will have no result." I believe it was not so much the deep condition of the country after the heavy rain as a recurrence of this fatal malady on the morning of Waterloo, added of course to the fact that he did not expect Blucher's arrival on the field of battle that day, which caused him to begin the action so late and so purposelessly to throw away hours which might have been employed in destroying Wellington before the Prussians could arrive. We know that during the progress of the battle itself he remained seated for hours motionless at a table placed for him in the open, often asleep with his head resting upon his arms; that also when flying beaten from the field he suffered so much from drowsiness it was with difficulty his attendants prevented him from tumbling from his horse. During the progress of the battle he was little on horseback, for riding caused him pain. He was thus debarred from seeing for himself much of the Prussian advance upon Planchenoit, and consequently did not fully realise what the dangers of his position were as early as he should have done had he been able to ride rapidly from point to point upon the field of battle to obtain information for himself. Indeed, it is to this cause only we can attribute the fact that he began this battle without having himself previously reconnoitred or examined Wellington's position, relying on General Haxo's report upon it.

Napoleon's character is a puzzle to most men and the composition of his brain is difficult to analyse. He had no real appreciation of what was beautiful in nature, felt little of the true poetry of life, and cared nothing for what we regard as virtue; but all we know of what he said or wrote regarding history in which he had no part, or about those who made it, or regarding the science of government, and the institutions and general machinery which keep civilised states going, displays wisdom and liberality. He thoroughly understood the minds and hearts of men, especially of Frenchmen, and was fully alive to those influences which form and mould the human character to make the individual either good or bad, and which, in doing so, make nations either great or little.

He knew full well how thoroughly he had satisfied French aspirations after military glory, but he could not have foreseen that what he did, together with the renown of his name, would have enabled a nephew in the next generation to bring about another Bonapartist Empire. If he be now conscious of what takes place on earth, how much the poignant remembrance of Waterloo must be salved by the knowledge (I judge from current French literature) that all which

Frenchmen care most still to remember of the past is directly connected with his immortal name! It was he who gave France the foremost position in Europe—a position the like of which no one nation before or since has ever occupied, and before which all European nations, England excepted, had humbly bent the knee. He found France in the throes of a foul, sanguinary revolution with all its horribly legalised crimes of murder and robbery, and from it, by his genius for government, he evolved order joined with progress. The fascination which in life he personally exercised over his own followers we often feel ourselves, even now, when we contemplate his soaring genius and attempt to measure his greatness.

For the part of the heroic conqueror, in which character he wished to be for ever remembered, death upon the battlefield was a necessity. Leonidas the Spartan, Epaminondas the Theban, Turenne the Frenchman, Wolfe and Moore the Englishmen, and above all of our national heroes the great Nelson,—all had fallen upon the field of their glory and their fame. Upon many remarkable occasions Napoleon showed his contempt of danger and how recklessly he could expose his own body when his doing so was calculated to help him to success. He knew how to win the imagination of Frenchmen and how with French armies to conquer; but he did not know how to die a hero's death. Why, oh why did he not end his days with those gallant souls who, when everything was lost, tried in his cause on the evening of that appalling overthrow to stem the overwhelming current of pursuit? Why did he not die with those who died for him upon that most eventful day of his life? But as a patriot how little worthy was he of all the

NAPOLEON AT ST. HELENA (*from a contemporary drawing*).

reverence and devoted love bestowed upon him by his brave, faithful and loyal army! It is as natural to die as to be born and it can matter little whether you fall like a soldier on the field of battle when young and vigorous, or "sicken years away" to die in your bed. If the average of human life were a hundred instead of thirty-three this question might be of some general importance; but it is not so. Bonaparte's march through the world was marked by the blood-trail of tens of thousands of gallant soldiers who, had it not been for his inordinate personal ambition, might have lived for years longer. Yet it is not for this reason or because he wasted upon horrible war the means of national prosperity and of individual enjoyment that men specially loathe his memory. It is because his whole career, from childhood to the day of his death, was one great untruth, and was made up of deceit, treachery, and the most appalling and selfish indifference to the feelings and wants of others—was, in fact, one great unholy deception. Even his most ardent admirers must freely admit that the great cause of Righteousness and of Peace never gained anything at his hands. A studied and finished actor in all his relations with men and women, he assumed at times an apparent kindly interest in the fate of those about him. He could even cleverly pretend a feeling of generous and magnanimous impulse when he thought it would pay him to do so. Throughout life he was always playing to an audience whether it were to his army by stirring general orders, or to France by lying bulletins, or to the world, present and to come, by his childish conduct at St. Helena and by the fictions he concocted there. The instrument he played upon was man, and no other human being has ever understood its gamut better or how to call forth its strong tones or to get more effect out of it. He knew the springs that moved man's moral machinery, especially the emotional side of humanity, and above all things the Frenchman's love of high-flown, melting sentiment. He was thus able to endear himself to France and especially to her splendid soldiers who loved him with a love the like of which we only find in the devotion with which the Tenth Legion loved Cæsar.

The name of this pre-eminently bad man fills a space in the world's history far greater than that occupied by all the men of action, all the thinkers, poets or writers of every age. Yet this man, who is still regarded by myriads as the greatest of human beings, failed in the mission he had set himself to accomplish—was even beaten at his own special trade—was declared an outlaw by all Europe, and died in prison. The public career of no great leader of men teaches us so painful a moral lesson upon the mockery of all earthly ambition, whilst the story of his private life indeed proclaims "how little are the Great." He died as he had lived, untruthful to the last. "Mene Mene, Tekel, Upharsin. God hath numbered thy kingdom, and finished it. Thou art weighed in the balances, and art found wanting." So wrote the finger on the wall about the proud King of Babylon. It might with equal truth have been written of him whose overthrow at Waterloo is thus described in verse:—

> "Since he miscalled the morning star,
> Nor man nor fiend hath fallen so far."

# INDEX.

ADAMS' brigade at Waterloo, 180
Alexander, Czar, 7, 8, 109; army for, 14, 17; Napoleon's misconception of his character, 29, 30; with Schwarzenberg's army in Bohemia, 55
Allemant, Marshals Marmont and Mortier driven back upon, 114
Allied armies in Germany, August 11, 1813, 54, 55
——————— march of Paris, 1814, 113–118
——— ———— in Waterloo campaign, 140–145
Archés, Napoleon hemmed in at, by the Allied Armies, 109, 111
Arcola, bridge of, Bonaparte at, 11
Augereau, Marshal, 10, 86, 88, 100
Austria; forces of, for the invasion of Russia, 9, 38, 39; assumes a position of armed neutrality, 40, 51, 72; and Italy, 99, 100

BACHELU's Infantry division, 152
Bagration, army of, 22
Bâle, column under Schwarzenberg at, 93
Barclay de Tolly's policy of cautious retreat, 18, 20, 21, 24, 25, 27; junction with the armies of Bagration at Smolensk, 22
Bar-sur-Aube, Marmont's corps falls back upon, 83
Bautzen, the Allies at, 46; battle of, 47–49
Bavarians, Napoleon and the, 69, 70; secession of, 99
Beauharnais, Prince Eugène de, 35, 38, 40, 86–88
Beaumont, Napoleon's headquarters at, 148
Belgium, Blucher's army in, 134, 135
Bellegrade, Austrian troops under, 88
Bennigsen, Russian army under, 69
Beresford at Bordeaux, 110
Beresina, the; Napoleon's retreating army at, 33
Berlin, Bernadotte's army at, 54, 55

Bernadotte; his army at Berlin, 54, 55; defeats French corps under Oudinot at Gross Beeren, 65, 66; defeats Ney at Dennewitz, 67; sends two corps to support Blucher's march on Paris, 100
Bernhard, Prince of Saxe-Weimar, 152
Berthier, Napoleon's Chief-of-Staff, 117
Blucher, Prince; Prussian army attacked by Ney at Bautzen, 48, 50; army under, in Silesia, 54–56, 58, 61; defeats French corps under Macdonald, 66, 67; Napoleon's repeated efforts to crush, 68, 69; column under, at Coblentz, 93; character of, 96; his march for Paris, 97–102; takes Soissons, 101, 102; battle of Laon, 104–106; army under, in Belgium, 134, 135, 140–142; inaccurate despatch of, 138; Napoleon's attack on June 15, 151–153; battle of Ligny, 153–163; wounded, 164; promises to support Wellington at Waterloo, 167, 168, 173
Bohemia, Schwarzenberg's army in, 54, 55
Bonaparte, Jerome, 159, 160
————, Joseph, defends Paris, 110, 111, 114; evacuates the city, 115
————, Lucien, 130
————, Napoleon, *see* Napoleon.
————, Victor, 41, 58, 83, 99
Borodino, battle of, between Napoleon and Kutusof, 27–29
Bourbons, the restoration of the, 119, 127, 133
Bourmont, General, 151
Brienne, indecisive action at, 98
Bülow, Prussian corps under, 100–102, 141, 153, 164, 165, 174, 175, 179

CAMPAIGN of 1813; Napoleon's scheme, 57, 58; account of, 37–74
———— of 1814, 6; the only defensive one waged by Napoleon, 81–92; disposition of his army, 83, 86; defends Paris against the Allies, 94–119; desertion of his generals, 118–120; Napoleon's strategy in, 125–6; composition of his army, 126, 127
———— of 1815; the hundred days, 128–193
Campo Formio, Treaty of, 3
Catalonia, French troops under Suchet in, 86, 89
Caulincourt, 129
Chalons, 112, 113; Victor's corps falls back upon, 83
Champ-Aubert, Russians destroyed at, 98
Character, Napoleon a bad judge of, 30
Charleroi, 148, 149
Charenton, Marshals Marmont and Mortier at, 114

# INDEX.

Chaumont seized by Napoleon's cavalry, 115
Coblentz, Blucher at, 93
Coburg, Napoleon's army at, 40
Colborne (Lord Seaton), 180
Compans, General, 112, 115
Conscription, the, in France, 1814, 9, 10, 84
"Continental system," designed for the purpose of destroying the commercial prosperity of England, 7-9; the inexpediency and unwisdom of, 84, 85
Craonne, Woronsoff defeated, 104

DANZIG, French garrison at, 55
Davoust, Marshal, 10, 40, 148; captures Hamburg, 47
Dennewitz, Ney defeated by Bernadotte at, 67
D'Erlon's corps, 148, 151, 152, 157, 161-163, 175, 176, 179
Desaix, Marshal, 10
Doulevent, Napoleon at, 116
Dresden; pageant of, May 1812, 13; Napoleon's triumphant entry into, 46, 47; battles round, in 1813, 61, 62, 67
Drissa, Russian camp at, 20

ELBA, Napoleon sent to, 121-125; escape from, 128
Elbe, French fortresses on the, 38, 70, 86
England, Napoleon's "Continental system" and, 7, 8; national debt during the invasion of Russia, 1812, 9; the Peninsula War, 53, 54; the "Hundred Days," 128-193
Epernay, Napoleon marches to, 108
Erfurth, Napoleon's army at, 40
Excelsman, cavalry of, 170

FÈRE-CHAMPENOISE, Marshal Marmont defeated at, 114
Ferté-sous-Jouarre, 101
Finland, army of, 30
Fontainbleau, Napoleon at, 117, 119
Fortifications, absence of, in Paris, 1814, 115
France, condition of, in 1814, 76, 77; enormous taxes in, 84; the conscription in, 9, 10, 84; manifesto issued to people of, by the Allies in 1814, 93; reconquered in 1815 without bloodshed, 132, 133; attack of Imperial Guard at Waterloo, 179, 180
Francis, Emperor, 40, 75, 88, 125; at Dresden, 13; with Schwarzenberg's army in Bohemia, 55; flees to Dijon, 113
Frankfort, the Allied Armies at, 75
Frasnes, village of, 152

GEMBLOUX, Grouchy at, 170, 171
Genappe, skirmish at, 171
Generals, Napoleon's, 10, 25, 37, 52, 117; inefficiency of, 42; treason of, 118, 119; force Napoleon to abdicate, 119-121
Gérard's corps of French troops destroyed by Bernadotte, 65; at Waterloo, 148, 149, 151, 159, 161, 163, 170, 181
Germany, Napoleon's new army in, 43; account of the 1813 campaign in, 43-74
Globokoë, 21
Gneisenau, Count, and the Prussian Short-Service System, 52; advises Blucher, 96, 163; friction with Wellington, 136, 137, 155, 156; orders the retreat upon Wavre, 164, 165; 174, 182
Gotha, Napoleon's army at, 40
Græme, Lieutenant, and the fall of La Haye Sainte, 178, 179
"Grand Army," for the invasion of Russia, 14, 27, 28; losses from sickness and desertion, 24; disastrous retreat from Moscow, 31-36; remains of, at Smorgoni, 33, 37, 38, 40
Gross Beeren, Bernadotte defeats Oudinot at, 65, 66
Grouchy, Marshal, 10, 140, 165; at Gembloux, 170, 171; movement on Wavre, 174, 181, 182; retreat to France, 183
Guard, Imperial, at Waterloo, attack of, 179, 180
Guignes, Napoleon at, 99

HAMBURG, captured by Davoust, 47; French garrison at, 55
Hamley, Sir E., on the campaign of 1814, 91
Heymès, Colonel, 178
Hill, Lord, corps of, 142
Holland joins the coalition against Napoleon in 1814, 93
Horses, want of, during the invasion of Russia, 21, 33
Hougoumont, attack upon, 175, 176

ITALY; Viceroy of, at Dresden, 13; troops from, join the remains of the "Grand Army," 35; Austria and, 99, 100

KATZBACH, the, Macdonald's army defeated by Blucher at, 66
Kellerman's corps of cavalry, 157
Kennedy, General, 178
Kovno, Napoleon's "Grand Army" at, 17; remains of, 33; bravery of Marshal Ney at, 34
Kulm, Vandamme's defeat at, 62-66
Kutusof, General, battle with Napoleon at Borodino, 27, 30; falls a victim to fever, 44

## INDEX.

LA HAYE SAINTE, fall of, 178, 179
La Rothière, Napoleon's defeat at, 98
La Vendée, 110
Laon, Bulow at, 101; battle of, 104-106
Leipzig, Napoleon's advance on, 44, 46; falls back on, 69; battle of, 69, 70
Louis XVIII., 128, 131, 133
Ligny, battle of 153-163, 165
Lithuania, Polish province of, 18
Loban's corps of French troops, 148, 171, 177
Lutzen, battle of, 45, 46, 49

MACDONALD, French corps under, 57, 61, 83, 99, 108; defeated by Blucher, 66, 67.
Madgeburg, remains of "Grand Army" at, 40
Marbot, General, 174, 175
Marmont, Marshal; corps of, falls back upon Bar-sur-Aube, 83; pursues Blucher, 98; attacked by Blucher, 101; defeated at the battle of Laon, 104, 105; retreat to Paris 114-119; desertion of Napoleon, 119, 120
Masséna, General, at Torres Vedras, 27
Mayence, Napoleon and the Bavarians at, 70
Metternich, and Schwarzenberg's movements, 96, 99, 100; flees to Dijon, 113
Military system of every great European Power in 1813, 43
Money, General, in command of the National Guard at Paris, 115
Mont St. Jean, 167; Wellington's forces fall back on, 171; attacked by Napoleon, 175
Moreau, General, surrenders Soissons, 101, 102
Mormant, the Allies surprised at, 99
Mortier, Marshal, French corps under, 83, 98, 111, 114, 116; at Soissons, 101, 102.
Moscow, distance from Smolensk, 26; entered by Napoleon, 29; capture of, 20, 27; Napoleon's disastrous retreat from, 31-36
Muffling, Baron, and Blucher, 96; and Wellington, 137-139, 167, 168
Murat, Marshal, 10, 26, 33, 37, 62

NAPOLEON, subject to periodic attacks of a mysterious malady, 1-3, 28, 29, 65, 74, 147, 148, 158, 159, 165, 168, 184-186; one of the greatest figures in history, 5; at Dresden in May 1812, 13; diplomatic difficulties, 14; plan of attack at Borodino, 28; a bad judge of character, 30; returns to France, [33; his invasion of

Russia ends in disastrous failure, 36; creation and organisation of a new army in Paris in 1813, 40-43; the peace negotiations at Prague, one of the most fatal mistakes made by, 51-53; army in August 1813, 55; scheme of campaign, 57, 58; rapid march to Dresden, 61, 67; and Vandamme, 65; efforts to secure the earliest and best intelligence of an enemy in time of war, 67, 68; repeated efforts to overwhelm Blucher, 68, 69; composition of his armies in 1812 and 1813, 71; mistakes made by, in 1813, 72, 73; his critical position at the opening of 1814, 75-80; return to Paris for fresh troops, 80; the nine weeks' campaign of 1814, the only defensive one waged by, 81-92; disposition of his army in 1814, 83, 86; the unwisdom and inexpediency of his "Continental system," 84, 85; defends his capital against the Allies in 1814, 94-119; rapid movements of, 106, 107; his project disclosed by an intercepted despatch, 112; desertion of his generals, 118-120; sent to island of Elba, 121-125; his strategy in the 1814 campaign, 125-127; escapes from Elba, 128; re-enters Paris, 129, 134; promulgates a form of Constitution, 130-132; prepares for the Waterloo campaign, 134, 135; mistakes made by, in 1815, 138, 139; his army, 140; plan of campaign, 144-149; attack on the Prussians, 151-153; battle of Ligny, 153-163; battle of Waterloo, 175-183; sent to St. Helena, 183; overthrow at Waterloo attributed to illness, 185-188; character of, 189-193

Nelson, victory at Trafalgar, 135

Ney, Marshall, 10; at the battle of Borodino, 29; bravery of, at Kovno, 34, 35; captures Torgau, 47; attack on the Allied Armies, 47, 48, 63; defeated by Bernadotte at Dennewitz, 77; his corps falls back upon Verdun, 83; joins Napoleon in 1815, 128; joins Napoleon near Charleroi, 151, 157; attack on Quatre Bras, 152, 159-164, 168, 171, 177, 178

Niemen River, "Grand Army" collected for the invasion of Russia, 14; passage of the, 17, 18; Marshal Ney covers the retreat across, 34

ODER, fortresses on the, 38, 70, 72
Orange, Prince of, corps of, 142
Orleans, Napoleon and, 117
Orleans, Duke of, 133
Orthez, Soult beaten by Wellington at, 110
Oudinot, French corps under, 57, 83, 99, 108; defeated by Bernadotte, 65
Ourousoff, Russians under, 98

PAJOL, cavalry of, 168, 170

Paris, Napoleon organises a new army in 1813, 40-43; returns to, in
    1814, for fresh levies, 80; his defence of, in 1814, 94-119;
    Napoleon's return to, from Elba, 128, 129
Peninsular War, the, 53, 54, 88, 89
Picton's division at Waterloo, 176
Piedmont, Napoleon's troops from, 87
Pirch, Prussian corps under, 141, 163, 179
Pire's cavalry corps, 152, 159
Planchenoit, Prussian attack at, 179, 181
Polish question, Napoleon and the, 19, 20
Poniatowski, French corps under, 58
Ponsonby's cavalry at Waterloo, 176
Prague, peace negotiations at, 51, 52
Prussia, King of, at Dresden, 13; with Schwarzenberg's army in
    Bohemia, 55
————, forces of, for the invasion of Russia, 9, 38, 39; swept of
    horses, 21; declares against Napoleon, 40; army attacked by Ney
    at Bautzen, 48, 50; effect of the peace negotiations at Prague on,
    51, 52

QUATRE BRAS, battle at, 149, 150, 159, 160-163, 171

REILLE's corps, 148, 151, 152, 157, 159, 168; attack upon Hougoumont, 175, 176
Rheims, General Priest takes, 107; recaptured by Napoleon, 107, 108
Rhine, Napoleon's army driven towards the, 70, 75, 82; the Allies
    cross the, 93
Ropes, Mr., articles on Waterloo, 173, 181
Russia; invasion of, in 1812: an appalling failure, 5-7, 36; military
    forces required for, 9; Napoleon's "Grand Army" collected on
    the Niemen, 14, 17, 71; and Poland, 19, 20; want of horses, 21;
    fighting near Smolensk, 24, 25; battle of Borodino, 27-29;
    Moscow entered, 29; Napoleon's disastrous retreat from Moscow,
    31-36; battle of Lutzen, 45; army attacked by Ney at Bautzen,
    49, 50; peace negotiations at Prague, 51, 52
Russians at Champ-Aubert, destroyed by Napoleon, 98

SAALFELD, Napoleon's army at, 40
Sacken, corps under, 98
St. Cyr, Marshal, 10, 58; holds Dresden, 61, 62
St. Dizier, Napoleon at, 113, 116
St. Helena, Napoleon sent to, 183, 191
St. Lambert, Bülow's corps at, 174, 175, 182

St. Priest, corps of, 100, 101; takes Rheims, 107; defeated by Napoleon, 107, 108
Saltoun, Lord, 180
Saxon contingent at the battle of Leipzig, 69
Saxony, secession of, 99; King of, at Dresden, 13, 46
Scharnhorst and the Prussian Short-Service System, 52
Schwarzenberg, Austrian army under, 38, 39; in Bohemia, 54-56; column under, at Bâle in 1814, 93; a timid strategist, 95, movements of, towards Paris, 96-99, 107-116; Metternich and, 96, 99, 100; attacked by Napoleon, 107-109
Seaton, Lord, 180
Secret societies at work in Central Europe, 1813, 49, 52
Ségur, Count de, 148
Silesia, Blucher's army in, 54-56
Smolensk, 17, 18, 22, 23; fighting near, 24, 25, 47; return march upon, 31, 33
Smorgoni, Napoleon leaves his army at, 33, 37, 38
Soissons, Wintzingerode's corps at, 100; town recaptured by Mortier, 101; surrenders to Blucher, 102, 103
Somerset's cavalry at Waterloo, 176
Soudé-Sainte-Croix, battle at, 113, 114
Soult and Wellington in the Peninsula, 86, 89, 95; defeated at Orthez, 110; army shattered at Toulouse, 122; chief of Imperial Staff, 157, 181
Spain, Wellington's victories in, 53, 54; Napoleon's army in, 88, 89
Stein, and the Prussian Short-Service System, 52; able statesmanship of, 92
Suchet, French troops held by, in Catalonia, 86, 89
Swedish army with Bernadotte at Berlin, 55
Switzerland joins the coalition against Napoleon in 1814, 93

TALLEYRAND summons the Allies to Paris, 116; and the restoration of the Bourbons, 119
Tchichagof, army of, 30
Thielmann, Prussian corps under, 141, 164, 165, 181
Thiers, M., the historian, on Moreau's surrender, 102, 103; on the 1814 campaign, 122, 126; on the overthrow of Napoleon, 181, 184, 185
Tilsit, alliance hatched at, 8
Torgau, Ney's capture of, 47
Toulouse, Wellington advances on, 110; Soult's army shattered at, by Wellington, 122
Trafalgar, Nelson's victory at, 135

# INDEX.

Treaty of Campo Formio, 3
Troyes, Napoleon at, 101
Turenne's battle at Entzheim, 63, 64
Tuscany, Napoleon's troops from, 87

UXBRIDGE, Lord, cavalry under, 142

VANDAMME, Marshal, 10, 58, 61, 181, 188; defeated at Kulm, 62-65
Vandamme's corps, 148, 151, 161, 162, 170
Vandeleur's cavalry brigades at Waterloo, 179, 180
Vauchamp, Blucher at, 98
Verdun, Ney's corps falls back upon, 83
Vienna, Congress of, 127
Vistula, fortresses on the, 38, 70, 72
Vittoria, battle of, 54, 88, 89
Vivian's cavalry brigade at Waterloo, 179, 180

WATERLOO campaign, full story of, yet to be written, 135; the French army, 140; armies of the Allies, 140-143; Napoleon's plans for, 144-149; account of the battle, 175-183
Wavre, retreat upon, 164-166, 174, 181
Weimar, Napoleon's army at, 40
Wellington, Duke of: defeat of Masséna at Torres Vedras, 27; and Napoleon's power in Europe at the beginning of 1812, 39; the Peninsular War, 53, 54, 88, 89; threatens Paris from the south, 76, 89; defeats Soult at Orthez, 110; sbatters Soult's army at Toulouse, 122; army of, in Flanders, 134, 135, 142, 143; friction with Count Gneisenau, 136-138; letter despatched by, to Blucher, 153, 154; attacked at Quatre Bras, 160-165; battle of Waterloo, 175-183
Wilna entered by Napoleon, 18, 19; departure from, 20; distance of Borodino from, 27; remains of the "Grand Army" at, 33
Wintzingerode's corps at Soissons, 100-102; sent to St. Dizier, 113; cavalry of, defeated by Napoleon, 116
Witepsk, Napoleon at, 20, 22, 23
Wittgenstein, Russian general, 44; battle of Lutzen, 45, 50
Woronzoff, corps of, 100; defeated at Craonne, 104
Wurtemberg, contingent at the battle of Leipzig, 69; secession of, 99

YORK, General, Prussian army under, 38, 39; column in Silesia, 56

ZIETHEN, Prussian corps under, 141, 151, 163; at Waterloo, 179-181

The attention of Military Readers

*IS SPECIALLY CALLED TO THE*

# Pall Mall Magazine

Edited by
LORD FREDERIC HAMILTON, M.P.,
and
SIR DOUGLAS STRAIGHT.

Price One Shilling.

*IN WHICH MANY*

## INTERESTING STUDIES upon MILITARY TOPICS

*REGULARLY APPEAR.*

No Club, Regimental Mess, or Military Reading-room is complete unless the Monthly PALL MALL MAGAZINE is included among its periodicals.

GENERAL LORD ROBERTS, V.C.,
 Has recently contributed a series of studies upon "WELLINGTON," fully illustrated from old Prints.

GENERAL VISCOUNT WOLSELEY, K.P.,
 Has contributed a valuable series of studies upon "THE DECLINE AND FALL OF NAPOLEON," fully illustrated with diagrams and maps.

LIEUT.-GEN. SIR EVELYN WOOD, V.C.,
 Has contributed studies upon "CAVALRY AT WATERLOO."

MR. RUDYARD KIPLING
 Has written for this Magazine several of his best "BARRACK-ROOM BALLADS."

MR. ARCHIBALD FORBES
 Has contributed popular Military Articles, full of interest.

The PALL MALL MAGAZINE may be obtained of any Bookseller at Home or abroad.

SUBSCRIPTION, including Postage, for One Year, 17s. 6d.

EDITORIAL AND PUBLISHING OFFICES: 18, CHARING CROSS ROAD, LONDON, W.C.

www.ingramcontent.com/pod-product-compliance
Lightning Source LLC
Chambersburg PA
CBHW020858230426
43666CB00008B/1227